Recipes for Balanced, Flexible, Feel-Good Meals

A Cookbook

Lilia S. Weingartner

BREAKFAST
Scrambled eggs with ham
Stewed fruits
Coffee

LUNCHEON
Canapé of sardines
Fried smelts, Tartar sauce
Broiled lamb chops
Stewed celery in cream
French fried potatoes
Vanilla custard pie

DINNER
Tuna fish salad
Chicken broth in cups
Queen olives
Roast capon, au cresson
French peas
Parisian potatoes
Lettuce salad, egg dressing
Fancy ice cream
Lady fingers
Coffee

Scrambled eggs with ham. Boiled ham cut in small dices and one small piece of butter. Put in vessel and add scrambled eggs. See plain scrambled eggs.

Canapé of sardines. Skin and split the sardines. Place on buttered toast, garnished with chopped eggs around the edges, and serve on napkin with quartered lemon and parsley in branches.

Fried smelts. Season the smelts, roll in flour, then in beaten eggs, and finally in bread crumbs. Fry in swimming fat and serve on napkin with fried parsley and lemons quartered. Sauce separate.

Fried parsley. Parsley in branches, well-washed and dried in towel. Fry in very hot swimming fat or lard for a second, as it fries very quickly. Salt and pepper. Can be used for garnishing fried fish and other dishes.

Tartar sauce. One chopped gherkin in vinegar, one tablespoonful of capers, a little chervil, parsley, chives and a tablespoonful of French mustard. Stir well into a cup of mayonnaise sauce.

Stewed celery in cream. Cut stalks or outside leaves of celery into one inch lengths. Wash well, parboil in salt water and allow to cool. Put back in salt water and boil until soft. Add one-half cup of cream sauce, a small piece of butter, one-half cup of cream, and season with salt and Cayenne pepper. Simmer for five minutes.

French fried potatoes. Cut raw potatoes in strips one-third inch thick and two inches long. Fry in swimming lard, but do not have it too hot. When potatoes are done remove from pan and let the fat become as hot as possible. Fry the potatoes again until they are a golden yellow. Remove, salt, and serve on a napkin. Do not cover, as this will cause them to become soft and spongy.

Tuna fish salad. (Thon mariné). This fish can be obtained in cans. Put in salad bowl some sliced lettuce with the tuna on top. Garnish with lettuce leaves and serve with French dressing. Do not mix until ready to serve.

Fancy ice cream. Fill fancy lead moulds with any kind of ice cream, using different colors in the same mould if desired. Cover with cracked ice and rock salt for thirty minutes. Remove and serve on doilies.

BREAKFAST
Strawberries in cream

DINNER
California oysters on shell

Oatmeal
Shirred eggs
Rolls   Coffee

LUNCHEON
Potato and leek soup
Broiled halibut steak, maître d'hôtel
Homemade beef stew
Lemon water ice
Fruit cake
Demi tasse

Consommé with sago
Écrevisses en buisson
Leg of veal, au jus
Browned mashed potatoes
Peas and carrots in cream
Hearts of lettuce, French dressing
Omelet with jelly
Coffee

SUPPER
Welsh rabbit

Shirred eggs, plain. Put eggs on buttered shirred egg dish and cook slowly. Salt and pepper.

Potato and leek soup. Simmer in butter one chopped onion and four stalks of leeks cut in small dices. When golden yellow add one tablespoonful of flour, mix, add one pound of potatoes cut in dices one-quarter inch square, one quart of stock or bouillon, and a bouquet garni. Boil until potatoes are done. Season with salt, pepper, a little grated nutmeg and chopped parsley.

Bouquet garni. Tie in a bundle a small piece of celery, of leek, and of parsley in branches, with a bay leaf, two cloves, a sprig of thyme, and, if desired, a clove of garlic, in the center. This is used for flavoring stews, soups, fish, etc.

Broiled halibut, maître d'hôtel. Cut halibut in slices one inch thick. Salt and pepper, dip in olive oil and broil. Serve with maître d'hôtel sauce, quartered lemon and parsley.

Homemade beef stew. Three pounds of rump, hip, or flank beef, cut into squares two inches thick. Season the meat and simmer in sauce pot with two chopped onions and three ounces of butter. When brown add two tablespoonsful of flour and simmer again. Then add hot water enough to cover the meat, and a bouquet garni. Cook for one hour and then add one pound of potatoes cut in squares one inch thick, and leave on fire until potatoes are soft. Take out the bouquet, add one cup of purée of tomatoes and boil for five minutes. Serve with a sprinkle of chopped parsley.

Consommé with sago. Bring one quart of consommé to a boil and then let one-third of a pound of sago run slowly into it. Cook for ten minutes.

Écrevisses en buisson. To three quarts of boiling water add one sliced onion, one carrot, a bouquet garni, one glassful of vinegar, and salt. Boil for five minutes. Then put in three dozen écrevisses, or crayfish, and boil for ten minutes. Serve on napkin with parsley and lemon, or serve in its broth if desired. For most écrevisses dishes the sauce is made "en buisson" first and then prepared in fancy fashion following.

Leg of veal, au jus. Put leg of veal in pan and treat same as roast veal. Baste often.

Browned mashed potatoes. Put in buttered egg dish some mashed potatoes. Sprinkle with grated Parmesan cheese, place a little butter on top, and bake in oven.

Peas and carrots in cream. Put in pot one pint of boiled peas, one pint of boiled French carrots, one cup of thick cream, salt and a pinch of sugar. Boil for a few minutes and thicken with a half cup of cream sauce.

Omelet with jelly. See omelet with strawberries. Roll the omelet in pan, put any kind of jelly in center, turn over on platter, and burn with hot iron.

BREAKFAST	AFTERNOON TEA	
Bananas and cream	Preserved strawberries toast	Dry
Force and cream	Chicken sandwiches	

Crescent rolls	Cocoa	Assorted cakes	Oolong tea

LUNCHEON	DINNER
Cream of potato soup	Purée of tomatoes, with rice
Radishes	Lobster Newburg
Broiled tenderloin steak, Bordelaise sauce	Roast chicken
Gendarme potatoes	Artichokes, Hollandaise
Asparagus tip salad	Waffle potatoes
Vanilla éclairs Demi tasse	Pistache ice cream
	Alsatian wafers Coffee

Forceandcream. Serve raw force on a compote dish, with cream and powdered sugar separate.

Creamofpotatosoup. Simmer a little sliced onion, leeks, celery, one bay leaf, a clove and a piece of pig skin, or a raw ham bone, in butter. Then add one cup of flour and simmer again. Pour in two quarts of boiling milk and two pounds of sliced raw potatoes and boil until the potatoes are soft. Season with salt and a little Cayenne pepper, and strain through a fine sieve. Before serving add the yolk of one egg mixed with a cup of thick cream, and stir in gradually three ounces of sweet butter.

Radishes. Wash well. The red skin of the turnip-shaped species may be cut back, beginning at the bottom point and extending toward the top, in the form of open leaves, to make them look like open roses, if desired. Serve on cracked ice.

Broiledtenderloinsteak. Salt and pepper the steak and dip in olive oil before broiling. Garnish with watercress and serve with maître d'hôtel sauce.

Bordelaisesauce. Simmer four shallots, chopped very fine, in two ounces of butter. When thoroughly warmed through add one-half glass of Bordeaux claret and reduce until nearly dry. Then add one pint of brown gravy and boil for five minutes. Then add one-quarter of a pound of sliced parboiled beef marrow, and a little chopped garlic, if that flavor is desired. Sprinkle with chopped parsley, and before serving stir in slowly two ounces of fresh butter. Serve poured over meats, or separate.

Gendarme potatoes. Peel some small potatoes and cut lengthwise in eight or more pieces. Put in roasting pan with salt, pepper and a piece of butter, and roast in oven for seven minutes. Add a sliced onion, mix well, and again roast, turning often.

Chicken sandwich. Slice boiled or left over roast chicken, very thin. Cut the bread thin and spread with sweet butter. Place the chicken between slices of the bread with a sprinkle of salt and pepper. Trim, and cut in shape desired.

Purée of tomato soup, with rice. Add one-half cup of boiled rice to each portion of purée of tomato soup.

Artichoke, Hollandaise. See [boiled artichokes](). Sauce Hollandaise served separate.

Lobster, Newburg. Cut the meat from the tails of California lobsters, in slices one-quarter inch thick. Put in sauté pan with butter, salt and pepper, and simmer for five minutes, or until the meat has a little color, over a quick fire. Then add for each lobster tail one cup of thick cream and one pony of brandy, and cook for two minutes. Thicken with yolks of two eggs mixed with a little cream, some very dry sherry wine, and a pinch of Cayenne pepper. Serve in chafing dish. Serve Madeira or sherry wine separate.

9

BREAKFAST	DINNER
Orange juice	Cream of chicken
Cream toast	Salted English walnuts
Coffee	Fillet of sole, Joinville

LUNCHEON

  Eggs au beurre noir
  Hamburg steak
  Lorraine potatoes
  Cole slaw, Thousand Island dressing
  Limburger cheese
  Rye bread and pumpernickle
  Coffee

  Roast tame duckling, apple sauce
  Sweet potatoes, Southern style
  Cold asparagus, mustard sauce
  Strawberry ice cream
  Cakes
  Coffee

SUPPER

  Chicken salad

Orangejuice. Strain the juice of peeled oranges through a napkin, and serve in glass surrounded with fine ice.

Eggsaubeurr enoir. Use soft-fried or shirred eggs. Put a piece of butter in hot frying pan and when nearly black and smoking add a dash of vinegar, and pour over the eggs. Drop a few capers and chopped parsley on top, and salt and pepper.

Hamburgsteak. To one and one-half pounds of trimmed beef, add four ounces of beef marrow, and pass through meat chopper, medium fine. Simmer some chopped onions in butter until nice and brown. Mix the meat and onions with salt, pepper, one raw egg, some chopped parsley, and a dinner roll soaked in water and chopped fine. Form the meat in round steaks one-half inch thick, roll in bread crumbs, and fry in pan in butter for about ten minutes. Remove the steaks carefully. Add a spoonful of flour to gravy in pan, simmer a little, and then add one-half cup of stock or water, pepper and salt, and strain before serving.

Lorrainepotatoes. Simmer one chopped onion and one-quarter pound of salt pork cut in small dices, in one ounce of butter, for five minutes. Then add three pounds of potatoes cut in pieces one inch square, one pint of stock or bouillon, salt and pepper, and a bouquet garni. Cook until soft and sprinkle with chopped parsley before serving.

ThousandIslanddr essing,forsalads. Two soupspoonfuls of mayonnaise, one soupspoonful of Chili sauce, one soupspoonful of French dressing, one teaspoonful of chopped pimentos, one-half teaspoonful of chopped olives, salt and pepper, all well mixed. Use a very cold salad bowl.

Cream of chicken. Place a soup hen in a soup kettle with three quarts of water, a leek, carrot, a little parsley and celery, six pepper berries, and two cups of rice. Boil until fowl is soft. Remove and cut away the white meat from the breast and set aside. Chop the remainder of the meat very fine, return to the kettle, and then strain the entire contents through a sieve. To the strained broth add one quart of milk, and strain again. Then add one-half pint of cream and the yolk of one egg, mixed; also a piece of sweet butter the size of an egg. Then add the breast of the fowl cut in small squares.

Roast tame duckling. See roast chicken. Also see stuffings.

10

BREAKFAST
　Shredded wheat biscuit
　Boiled eggs
　Rolls
　Coffee

LUNCHEON
　Holland herring
　Boiled potatoes
　Waffles and honey
　Coffee

DINNER
　Lynn Haven oysters on half shell
　Philadelphia pepper pot
　Roast canvas-back duck
　Hulled corn
　Currant jelly
　Cauliflower au gratin
　Celery mayonnaise
　Neapolitan ice cream

Assorted cakes

Demi tasse

Shreddedwheatbiscuits. Put the biscuit in a deep dish. A little boiling water poured over it will enable you to economize on cream.

Philadelphiapepperpot. Simmer in kettle four large onions chopped fine, one piece of celery, two leeks, one green pepper cut in very small squares, and one-quarter pound of butter. When done add two soupspoonsful of flour, and simmer again; add two quarts of stock, two pounds of tripe and one pound of potatoes cut in small squares, a bouquet garni and salt. Cook for two hours. Before serving remove the bouquet garni, add a tablespoonful of fresh-ground pepper, a little chopped parsley and some flour dumplings. Let the flour dumpling dough run through an ordinary sieve into boiling water and boil for just a minute.

Flourdumplings. One cup of flour, two eggs, three-fourths of a cup of milk, salt, and a little nutmeg. Mix well. Pass through colander with holes of about one-third inch in diameter, into boiling salt water. Boil for about three minutes, drain off water, put on platter and pour some brown butter over them.

Brownbuttersauce. Put good-sized piece of sweet butter into frying pan and allow to brown. May be served poured over the dish, or in separate sauce bowl.

Hulledcorn. May be obtained in cans. Follow directions on same. To hull corn is quite a complicated process, requiring the use of lye, etc.

Canvas-backduck. Same directions as for teal duck. Roast for about eighteen minutes.

Celerymayonnaise. Cut raw celery in strips like matches and wash well, then put in napkin on cracked ice, so it will become crisp. Serve with well-seasoned mayonnaise sauce, either on top or separate, as desired.

Poundcake. One-half pound of butter, one-half pound of sugar, one-half pound of flour, five eggs, a little rum and a teaspoonful of baking powder. Beat the butter with sugar until white, add the eggs one by one, while beating briskly. Mix the flour and the baking powder in together, and last of all add the rum. Put in mould and bake in oven for one hour.

Fruit cake. To the pound cake batter add one-half pound of chopped mixed glacé fruits, and one-half pound of raisins.

11

BREAKFAST
  Pearl grits and cream
  Fried eggs
  Rolls
  Chocolate

LUNCHEON
  Cold assorted meats
  Potato salad
  Iced tea

AFTERNOON TEA
  Chicken à la King
  Bread and butter sandwiches
  Raspberry water ice
  Champagne wafers
  Almond cake
  Tea
  Chocolate
  Whipped cream

DINNER
  Consommé with tapioca
  Boiled salmon, mousseline sauce
  Potatoes Hollandaise
  Roast goose, apple sauce
  St. Francis potatoes
  Celery Victor
  Baked Alaska
  Coffee

Pearl grits with cream. See hominy in cream.

Potato salad. Slice three boiled potatoes while hot. Add one small onion chopped fine, some chopped parsley, salt and pepper, two spoonsful of olive oil, and one each of boiling bouillon, or boiling water, and vinegar. Mix carefully so as not to break the potatoes, and serve in salad bowl with lettuce garnishing.

Chicken à la King. Take the breast of a boiled chicken or hen (fowl), and cut in very thin, diamond-shape pieces. Put in pan and add three-quarters of a pint of cream, salt and Cayenne pepper. Boil from three to five minutes. Add a glass of best sherry or Madeira wine. Boil for a minute and thicken with the yolks of two eggs, mixed with one-quarter pint of cream. Put some sliced truffles on top.

Raspberry water ice. One-half pound of sugar, one pint of water, and one pint of fresh raspberry pulp strained through a fine sieve. Squeeze in the juice of one lemon, add a little coloring if desired, strain and freeze.

Consommé with tapioca. To one quart of boiling consommé add slowly one cup of tapioca, and boil for eight minutes.

Bread and butter sandwiches. Spread sweet butter on thin slices of bread, and place face to face in pairs. Cut in any fancy shape, or roll and tie with soft baby ribbon.

BREAKFAST
- Honey in comb
- Boiled eggs
- Postum cereal
- Dry toast

DINNER
- Oyster soup, family style
- Salted English walnuts
- Fried chicked, country style
- Au gratin potatoes
- Cauliflower, Polonaise

LUNCHEON

Cold goose and Virginia ham

Port de Salut cheese

Crackers

Coffee

Escarole and chicory salad

Chocolate profiterole

Coffee

SUPPER

Canapé regalia

Postum cereal. A prepared breakfast food obtainable from all grocers. Follow directions on package.

Oyster soup, family style. Boil two dozen oysters with their juice. In a separate vessel boil one quart of milk and one pint of cream. Put both together and add two ounces of sweet butter, and salt and pepper. Before serving stir in some fine cut chives and one-half cup of broken crackers.

Au gratin potatoes. Fill a shallow buttered dish with hashed in cream potatoes. Sprinkle with grated Parmesan cheese, put a little butter on top, and bake in oven until brown.

Cauliflower, Polonaise. Put on a platter some fresh-boiled cauliflower and sprinkle with two finely chopped boiled eggs, salt and pepper and some chopped parsley. In a pan on range put three ounces of sweet butter. When warm add two tablespoonsful of fresh bread crumbs and allow to become well browned. Pour over cauliflower when very hot.

Fried chicken, country style. Put the dressed chicken in salt water and leave for about one hour. Then wash and dry between towels, season with pepper and a small amount of salt, and dredge well with flour. Place in frying pan about three tablespoonsful of lard and two or three slices of fat breakfast bacon. When bacon is brown remove, and strain the lard, being careful that it is not burned. Have the lard very hot and fry the chicken. When brown, and well done, remove the chicken and strain the lard again through a hair sieve, then return lard to range, and stir in thoroughly one tablespoonful of flour, being careful to have no lumps. Immediately before serving stir into the sauce one pint of cream, and let boil for one minute. Dress with the bacon and parsley in branches.

Canapé Regalia. Regalia is a special fish paste obtainable in cans. To one small can add two ounces of butter, mix well, and spread on fresh toast. Garnish with chopped eggs, serve on napkin with lemon in quarters and parsley in branches.

13

BREAKFAST
  Bananas and cream
  Scrambled eggs with chives
  Dry toast
  Coffee

LUNCHEON
  Pickled oysters
  Consommé in cups
  Broiled bluefish, maître d'hôtel
  Tripe, Lyonnaise
  Mashed potatoes
  Hearts of lettuce, egg dressing
  Chocolate éclairs
  Demi tasse

DINNER
  Potage Cambridge
  Boiled sheepshead, Hollandaise sauce
  Potatoes nature
  Chicken, Diva
  French peas
  Endive salad
  Strawberries with cream
  Assorted cakes
  Corn bread, Maryland
  Coffee

Pickled oysters. Parboil one carrot and one celery root cut in strips, and one onion sliced fine. Pour off water and finish cooking in one glassful each of white wine, and white wine vinegar, with a spoonful of pepper berries tied in cheese cloth. When done remove the peppers, add three dozen oysters and bring to a boil. Serve cold with parsley.

Broiled bluefish. Split the bluefish, remove the bones, season with salt and pepper, dip in oil and broil. Serve maître d'hôtel sauce on top, and quartered lemons and parsley.

Boiled sheepshead, Hollandaise sauce. Same as boiled salmon, Hollandaise.

Maryland corn bread. Beat two eggs until very light, and stir in one pint of sweet milk. Then sift one-half pint of coarse corn meal, add a teaspoonful of yeast powder, half a teaspoonful of salt, and a tablespoonful of melted lard or butter. Stir this into the milk and eggs. Mixture must be a thin batter. Bake in small bread pan or muffin rings.

Chicken, Diva. Prepare the chicken as for roast and stuff with rice stuffing. Put chicken in kettle and cover with stock or water. When done prepare a suprême sauce with the stock, pour over the chicken, and sprinkle with chopped Virginia ham. Carve at table.

Rice stuffing. Simmer a small chopped onion in butter, add one cup of washed rice, three cups of stock or bouillon, season, and cook in oven for twenty minutes. Then add two truffles cut in small squares. This stuffing is used for poultry, game, peppers, tomatoes, etc.

Suprême sauce. Melt three ounces of butter, add two ounces of flour, and simmer, but do not allow to brown. Add one and one-half pint of chicken stock, reduce for ten minutes, thicken with the yolk of one egg, a cup of cream and a small piece of sweet butter. Season with salt and a little Cayenne pepper. This sauce may be used with many entrée dishes.

Potage Cambridge (soup). Melt three ounces of butter in vessel, add two ounces of flour, and simmer for five minutes, or until golden yellow. Add one pint of veal broth or stock, one-half pint of purée of tomatoes and the trimmings of a few fresh mushrooms. Cook for twenty minutes, strain through sieve and add fine-cut strips of fresh mushrooms sauté in butter. A pony of dry sherry wine may be added if desired.

Strawberry ice cream. One pint of cream, one quart of milk, the yolks of eight eggs, one-half pound of sugar, one pint of strawberry pulp or strained strawberries, the juice of one lemon and a little coloring. Put the milk with half the sugar on the fire to boil. Mix the remainder of the sugar with the eggs, stir the boiling milk into it, and cook until it becomes creamy, but do not allow it to boil. Remove from the fire, add the cream, strawberry pulp and lemon juice, cool and freeze.

14

BREAKFAST
- Grapefruit with vanilla sugar
- Finnan haddie in cream
- Puff paste crescents
- Oolong tea

LUNCHEON
- Green onions
- Radishes
- Eggs ministerielle
- Vermicelli aux croutons
- Cold asparagus, mustard sauce
- Cup custard
- Coffee

DINNER
- Clam chowder, Manhattan style
- Queen olives
- Fillet of sole, Marguery
- Omelet with spinach
- Broiled fresh mushrooms
- Coffee ice cream
- Assorted cakes
- Demi tasse

Puff paste crescents. Two pounds of flour, one pound of butter, one pint of milk, one ounce of salt, one and one-half ounces of sugar and two ounces of yeast dissolved in warm water. Mix one-half pound of the flour with one-half pint of water and the dissolved yeast. Stand in warm place for about twenty minutes. Put the remainder of flour on board and mix in the yeast paste; when sufficiently risen, add salt, sugar and milk, make a stiff dough and allow to stand for a few minutes. Roll out, put the butter into the dough as for ordinary puff paste, and roll in the same way, but giving it only half the number of turns.

Stock for soup. Two pounds of beef bones and a marrow bone, if you can obtain one, two gallons of water, a carrot, onion, leek, piece of parsley, a bouquet garni, salt and pepper. Boil for three hours. Strain.

Puff paste (feuilletage). Take one pound of flour and one cup of water and make a smooth paste, but not too soft. Form into a square loaf and let it set for about fifteen minutes. Roll out on floured board about one-half inch thick, and place in the center one pound of butter, well-worked and flexible. Fold the edges of the paste over the butter and roll out about one-quarter inch thick, taking care that the butter does not run out of the dough. Brush off the flour and fold in three. Roll out again to the same thickness as before and repeat the folding. Put in cool place or ice box for about one-half hour, then roll and fold as before. Again rest for one-half hour, and then roll and fold again. The paste will then have six turns in all, and after a little rest it can be used.

Brown gravy. One pound of veal bones, cut in pieces and browned in oven, with one carrot, one onion, a little thyme, one bay leaf, two cloves and three ounces of butter. Baste well, then add three ounces of flour, allow to brown a little, and then add two quarts of water and boil for two full hours. Season with salt, and strain. This gravy is used as a foundation for many fancy sauces, such as sauce Madère, etc.

BREAKFAST
  Stewed rhubarb
  Grape-nuts with cream
  Yarmouth bloaters
  Rolls
  Coffee

LUNCHEON
  Shrimp salad
  Lamb chops
  Julienne potatoes
  French string beans
  Chocolate macaroons
  Coffee

DINNER
  Seapuit oysters on half shell
  Onion soup au gratin
  Salted pistachio nuts
  Whitefish, maître d'hôtel
  Sweetbreads braisé, au jus
  Purée St. Germain
  Olivette potatoes
  Roast leg of lamb, mint sauce
  Romaine salad
  Pineapple punch
  Lady fingers
  Coffee

Stewed rhubarb. Peel one pound of rhubarb, cut in two inch pieces, and place in shallow pan. Put on top one-quarter pound of sugar, a small piece of cinnamon, and one-half pint of water. Cover and put in oven for about twenty minutes. Remove, take out the cinnamon, and serve cold in its own juice. Cream and powdered sugar separate.

Grape-nuts with cream. Serve as prepared in package. Cream and powdered sugar separate.

Yarmouth bloater. Imported in cans. Put on broiler and heat through. Serve with maître d'hôtel sauce, quartered lemons and parsley.

Shrimp salad. Season fresh-boiled shrimps with salt, pepper and a little vinegar. Put some sliced lettuce in the bottom of a salad bowl, lay the shrimps on top, and cover with mayonnaise sauce. Garnish with quartered hard boiled eggs, fancy-cut beets, capers and queen olives. Serve very cold.

Julienne potatoes. Cut raw potatoes in thin strips like matches, and full length of potatoes. Fry in swimming fat, lard preferred, until crisp. Remove from fat, salt, and serve on napkin. Do not cover.

Onion soup, au gratin. Simmer three very finely sliced onions in butter until brown. Add one cup of bouillon or consommé, and boil for a few minutes. Put in earthern pot, or petite marmite, and place some slices of toasted French bread, previously prepared, on top. Put one-half cup of grated Parmesan cheese on the bread, set in very hot oven, and bake until the cheese is browned. Season to taste.

Whitefish, maître d'hôtel. Split the fish and remove the bones. Salt, pepper, dip in oil and broil. Serve with maître d'hôtel sauce, quartered lemons and parsley.

Purée St. Germain (vegetable). Strain cooked peas through a fine sieve. Put in pan with a piece of butter, salt and a pinch of sugar. Stir well, and when hot, add a very little thick cream. The purée should be firm, like mashed potatoes.

16

BREAKFAST
  Stewed prunes

  Malta Vita with cream

  Poached eggs on toast
  Rolls

LUNCHEON
  Hors d'oeuvres variés

  Fried fillet of sole, rémoulade sauce

  Broiled quail on toast
  Chiffonnade salad

Coffee   Soufflée potatoes
                                            Savarin au fine champagne
                                            Demi tasse

DINNER

Cotuit oysters on half shell
Petite marmite   Salted almonds
Terrapin, Maryland style
Roast ribs of beef
Stewed tomatoes   Mashed potatoes
Cold artichokes, mustard sauce
English breakfast tea ice cream
Assorted cakes   Coffee

Stewed prunes. Wash well one pound of prunes, and soak in cold water for two hours. Put on fire in same water, add a small piece of cinnamon stick, the peel of a quarter of a lemon, and two ounces of sugar, and cook on slow fire until soft. It will require about one hour. If an earthern pot with cover is used, put in bake oven for about two hours. The flavor will be better.

Malta Vita. Serve with powdered sugar, and cream, separate.

Hors d'oeuvres variés. (Appetisers assorted). Hors d'oeuvres are different delicacies, and, except in rare instances, are served cold. They consist of caviar, pickled oysters, Lyon sausages, any kind of fish salad, pâté de foie gras, smoked salmon, smoked goose breast, and many others. From one dish to two dozen kinds may be served, allowing the guests to make a selection. Each kind should be served on a separate platter, or silver bowl.

Caviar. Leave the caviar three hours on ice. Serve in a glass dish. For each person have a round platter with napkin, a lettuce leaf filled with fine chopped onion and a quarter of a lemon. Thin dry toast and sweet butter separate.

Pâté de foie gras. (Goose liver patty.) Obtainable in cans or terrines, of different sizes. Remove the fat, which is put on top as a preservative, and with a soup spoon, which has been dipped in hot water, cut the paste in thin slices, and serve on lettuce leaves on a napkin. Garnish with meat jelly and parsley in branches. Let the pâté de foie gras stand in ice box a few hours before opening and serving.

Lyon sausage. A kind of imported beef sausage. Slice thin.

Stuffed eggs. Cut hard boiled eggs in two, either way. Mix the yolks with equal parts of sweet butter and pass through a sieve. Add salt, paprika, a little anchovy paste, and some chives. Mix well, and fill the halved eggs. Or the yolks may be mixed with butter, and some poppy or celery seeds, etc. Also with any kind of purée, such as purée of tomatoes, regalia, chicken, etc. If the filling is put in a pastry bag with a star mould in the bottom, to squeeze it through, the eggs can be filled in an attractive and novel manner. Serve very cold.

Sardines. Serve cold with quartered lemons, on lettuce leaves.

Sliced tomatoes. Have the tomatoes very cold. Peel and slice, and serve on lettuce leaves, with French dressing. To peel, put tomatoes in hot water for ten seconds, and peel immediately.

17

BREAKFAST
Baked apples
Boiled eggs
Toast
Coffee

LUNCHEON
Grapefruit with cherries
Steak and kidney pie
Cream cheese
Maryland beaten biscuits

DINNER
Consommé Madriléne
Ripe California olives
Sand dabs, meuniére
Butterball duck with currant jelly

>   Fried hominy
>   French endive salad
>   Asparagus, Hollandaise
>   Fancy ice cream
>   Assorted cakes
>   Coffee

Grapefruit with cherries. Cut the grapefruit in two pieces. Split some maraschino cherries and decorate. Pour a little maraschino on top.

Steak and kidney pie. Use individual pie dishes. A slice of raw sirloin steak one-half inch thick, cut in two. Two lamb kidneys cut in two. Salt, pepper, and roll in flour, put in pie dish and cover with a little cold water. Cover with piecrust dough and bake in oven for about eighteen minutes. Serve in the dishes in which they were baked, on napkins.

Butterball duck. Roast in hot oven for about twelve minutes.

Assorted cakes. Any kind of small cakes. Serve on a compotier, on doily. The more varied the assortment the better.

Maryland beaten biscuits. To one pint of sifted flour add one heaping teaspoonful of lard, or butter, and a little salt. Mix with one pint of sweet milk to stiff dough. Beat with a mallet for one hour. The success of same depends upon the beating. Shape as for tea biscuits and bake.

Macaroons. Mix one pound of almond paste with one pound of powdered sugar. Add the whites of six eggs and a spoonful of flour and mix well. Squeeze through a pastry bag onto paper, moisten the tops with water, using a brush, and bake in a very slow oven for about twenty minutes.

Lady fingers. Eight eggs, with the yolks and whites separate, one-half pound of sugar, one-half pound of flour, and some vanilla flavoring extract. Beat the sugar with the yolks until light; then beat the whites very stiff. Mix the flour with the yolks and sugar, then add the beaten whites and mix lightly. Dress on paper with a plain pastry bag, in the shape wanted. Dust powdered sugar on top and bake in a moderate oven.

BREAKFAST
  Guava jelly
  Oatmeal with cream
  Rolls
  Coffee

LUNCHEON
  Mariniert herring
  Plain boiled potatoes
  Calf's liver, sauce piquante
  Fried egg plant
  Oregon cream cheese and crackers
  Coffee

DINNER
  Purée of game, hunter style
  Salted English walnuts
  Roast capon
  Compote of pears
  Stewed celery, au Madère
  Paille potatoes
  Bavarois à la vanille
  Fancy macaroons
  Coffee

Mariniert herring. Soak six salt herrings in water for twelve hours. Then put in pot with one sliced onion, some whole parsley, a spoonful of whole black pepper berries, three bay leaves and six cloves. Mix one teaspoonful of English mustard with a cup of vinegar and pour over herring. Cover all with thick cream, shake well to thoroughly mix, and let stand for two days before serving. Serve with thin slices of one lemon on top, or, if desired, the lemon may be put with the herring for a day.

Calf's liver, sauté. Slice the liver one-quarter inch thick, salt, pepper, roll in flour and fry in butter. Do not fry too long as it will make the liver tough. Serve on a platter with its own gravy, chopped parsley, and quartered lemons.

Sauce piquante. Simmer one chopped onion with a piece of butter. Add two spoonsful of crushed pepper berries and half a glass of vinegar. Reduce almost dry. Then add one pint of brown gravy, boil for fifteen minutes, and strain. Chop fine one-half cup of gherkins, put into the sauce and boil for a few minutes. Add a sprinkle of chopped parsley.

Fried egg plant. Peel and cut the egg plant into slices one-quarter of an inch thick. Salt, pepper, roll in flour, then in beaten eggs, and finally in bread crumbs. Fry in swimming lard, fat, or butter. Place on napkin, sprinkle with a little more salt, and garnish with parsley.

Purée of game soup. Simmer the carcasses or meat of almost any kind of game, such as duck, rabbits, hares, venison, bear, etc. Cut in pieces and add one carrot, an onion, two bay leaves, two cloves, a piece of celery, a little thyme, some pepper berries and four ounces of butter. Roast all together until nice and brown. Add a cup of flour and simmer again until the flour is of a brownish color. Then add one and one-half quarts of bouillon, or stock, and boil for an hour. Strain, pressing all the soft parts of the game through the sieve, and season with salt and Cayenne pepper. Before serving add one-half glass of dry sherry wine or Madeira.

Purée of game, St. Hubert. Add to above soup some square cut pieces of roasted game, before serving.

Stewed celery, au Madère. Wash well and cut the celery stalks in pieces one inch long. Parboil in salt water, cool, and put back to boil in enough stock to cover. When nearly done drain off most of the stock, add a cup of brown gravy, and boil until soft. Salt and pepper, and add a little dry sherry or Madeira before serving.

Paille potatoes (straw). Cut in thin strips like straws the full length of the potato. Fry in very hot lard, serve in napkin, and salt when first removed from fat.

Fancy macaroons. Mix one pound of almond paste, three-quarters of a pound of powdered sugar, the whites of five eggs and one spoonful of flour. Put in pastry bag with a fancy tube and squeeze the paste through, about the size of a half dollar. Put half of a glacé cherry on top and let stand over night in a dry place. Bake in oven for ten minutes.

BREAKFAST
  Stewed apples
  Pettijohns with cream
  Ham and eggs
  Dry toast
  Oolong tea

LUNCHEON
  Canapé Riga
  Planked smelts, en bordure
  Sirloin steak, sauce Colbert
  Haricots panachés
  Lettuce and tomato salad
  Pistache éclairs
  Coffee

DINNER
  Potage santé
  Salted pecans
  Crab meat, au beurre noisette
  Roast tame duckling, apple sauce
  Corn fritters and potato croquettes
  Waldorf salad
  Fancy ice cream
  Assorted cakes
  Coffee

Canapé Riga. One-half tuna fish (thon mariné) and one-half caviar mixed. Spread on thin toast, buttered. Decorate around the edges with chopped eggs, quartered lemon and parsley in branches.

Planked smelts, en bordure. Split some large smelts down the back and remove the bones. Place on a buttered plank with salt, pepper and a little butter on top. Put some potato, prepared as for potato croquettes, into a pastry bag with a star tube, and press out a border around the fish about an inch high. Put in oven and bake for about fifteen minutes. Serve with a little maître d'hôtel butter on top, and garnish with quartered lemons and parsley.

Sauce Colbert. Chop three shallots very fine, and simmer in butter. Add one-half glass of claret, and reduce almost dry. Then add one pint of brown gravy and cook for ten minutes. Before serving add three ounces of sweet butter, the juice of one lemon, and some chopped parsley.

Potage santé (soup). Wash a good handful of sorrel and slice very thin. Put in pot with three ounces of butter and simmer slowly for ten minutes. Then add one quart of bouillon, or consommé, and boil for a few minutes. Thicken with the yolks of two eggs mixed with a cup of cream. Before serving put in some French bread, or rolls, that have been dried in the oven, and cut like chip potatoes.

Boiled crabs. Put two live crabs in a pot and cover with cold water. Add one glass of white wine vinegar, an onion, carrot, a bouquet garni and salt. Boil for thirty-five minutes and let become cool without removing from the water. Serve cracked, cold, with mayonnaise or any kind of cold sauce; or remove from shell and serve as a salad; or prepare hot in many ways.

Crab meat, au beurre noisette. Put some fresh-boiled crab meat on a platter and season with salt and pepper. In a frying pan put a quarter pound of sweet butter. Simmer until of a hazel color, and pour over crab meat. Sprinkle with chopped chervil, or parsley, on top, and garnish with lemon.

Waldorf salad. Half white celery and half apple, cut in small squares. Put both in salad bowl, but do not mix. Cover with mayonnaise and season to taste.

BREAKFAST	LUNCHEON
Honey in comb	Eggs Marigny
Waffles	French pastry
Kippered herring	Iced tea
Baked potatoes	

Rolls and coffee

DINNER

Consommé Cialdini
Radishes
Fillet of bass, 1905
Larded sirloin of beef, Richelieu
Salade Doucette
Meringue glacée, Chantilly
Coffee

Eggs Marigny. Put in a buttered cocotte dish a very thin, small, slice of ham, with two parboiled oysters on top. Break an egg over all, salt, pepper, cover with cream sauce and a little grated cheese, and bake in oven until done.

Consommé Cialdini. Cut some carrots, turnips and potatoes, with a fancy cutting spoon, to the size of a large pea. Cook each separate in salt water. When done put in consommé and add the boiled white meat of chicken cut in small squares, a few boiled or canned peas, and some chervil. Serve separate some very thin slices of French bread or rolls.

Larded sirloin of beef. Remove the skin and fat of the sirloin, half way near the thick part. Lard same and roast in the usual manner.

Richelieu. A garnish for beef and other meats. Is prepared in various styles. Here are four good ones.

Stuffed tomatoes with rice Créole, stuffed fresh mushrooms à la D'Uxelles, braised lettuce and potatoes château.

Tomatoes, whole and baked, string beans, mushrooms and potatoes château.

Bouquet of all kinds of vegetables, fillets of anchovies, mushrooms and green olives.

Buttons of artichokes stuffed, stuffed tomato, mushrooms, lettuce braisé and potatoes château.

Fillet of bass, 1905. I originated this style in 1905, hence the name. Cut fillets of any kind of bass in pieces about three inches square, and free from skin and bones. Place on a piece of toast in a buttered shirred egg dish; salt, pepper, and place three nice heads of fresh mushrooms sauté in butter, on top of the fish. Put a soupspoonful of maître d'hôtel butter on top of the mushrooms, cover with a glass globe and bake in oven for twenty minutes. Just before serving uncover the fish, pour a little white wine sauce on top, re-cover, and serve.

Salade Doucette. Field salad.

Meringue glacée, Chantilly. Same as meringue glacée à la vanille. But decorate with whipped cream, passed through a pastry bag with a star tube.

21

BREAKFAST
  Bar le Duc jelly

  Horlick's malted milk

  Boiled eggs

  Maryland beaten biscuits

LUNCHEON
  Stuffed eggs

  Broiled salmon steak, anchovy butter

  Olivette potatoes

  Breaded lamb chops, Milanaise

  Pickled beets

  German apple cake   Coffee

DINNER
  Seapuit oysters on shell
  Consommé royal
  Skatefish au beurre noir   Potatoes nature
  Roast top sirloin of beef, forestière   Yorkshire pudding

Chiffonnade salad

Fancy ice cream   Assorted cakes   Coffee

Stuffed eggs with crab meat. Cut in two some hard-boiled eggs and remove the yolks. Fill the whites with fine-chopped crab meat mixed with a very thick mayonnaise. Chop the yolks and mix with a little chopped parsley, and sprinkle over the eggs. Serve very cold.

Broiled salmon steak. Cut a slice of salmon about one inch thick, salt, pepper, dip in oil and broil. Serve on platter with maître d'hôtel sauce, and garnish with quartered lemons and parsley in branches. Or serve with anchovy butter or other sauce, either on top or separate.

Anchovy butter. Fresh butter mixed with anchovy paste and the juice of a lemon.

Breaded lamb chops. Salt and pepper the chops, roll in flour, then in beaten eggs, then in bread crumbs, and fry in butter.

Spaghetti Milanaise. Boiled spaghetti cut in two inch lengths, a slice of boiled ham, a slice of tongue, six mushrooms and one truffle cut in strips the same size as the spaghetti. Put all in one pot, add a little tomato sauce, salt and pepper, and let simmer for a few minutes. Serve grated Parmesan cheese separate. If served as a garnish with "lamb chops, Milanaise," mix the cheese before serving.

Consommé Royal. Beat four eggs and season well. Add one pint of warm (not hot), consommé, put in a buttered mould and set in a pan of hot water. Cook slowly in a moderate oven. When the custard is done allow to cool, and cut in any shape desired. Serve hot consommé, with royal custard as a garnish.

Skatefish au beurre noir. Place the skate in boiling water for a few minutes, when the skin may readily be scraped off. Put in cold water, add a little milk to make the fish white, salt, and bring to a boil. Take off the fire, but leave in the water for ten minutes. Then put fish on platter, salt, pepper, sprinkle with a little vinegar, a few capers and some chopped parsley. Put in frying pan a quarter pound of butter, allow to become almost black, and pour over fish.

Roast top sirloin of beef. Same as roast sirloin of beef.

Forestière, for sauce. Sliced fresh mushrooms, simmered in butter. Add brown gravy and boil for ten minutes. Before serving stir in a little sherry wine.

Yorkshire pudding. One cup of milk, one-half cup of flour, two eggs, and one teaspoonful of baking powder. Mix well, add salt, pepper and one-half cup of chopped beef suet. Bake in roasting pan with beef fat from your roast. When done cut in squares.

22

BREAKFAST
  Grapefruit
  Germea with cream
  Crescents
  Cocoa

LUNCHEON
  Scrambled eggs, Morocquaine
  Lamb trotters, poulette
  Potatoes St. Francis
  Moka éclairs
  Tea

DINNER
  Bisque of clams
  Frogs' legs, sauté à sec
  Tournedos Massenet
  Jets de houblons
  Endives au cerfeuil
  Mince pie
  American cheese
  Coffee

Germea and cream. Powdered sugar and cream separate.

Scrambled eggs, Morocquaine. Cut cèpes in small squares, fry in butter and place in middle of scrambled eggs. Tomato sauce around the edge.

Lamb trotters, poulette. Cook lambs' feet in stock or water with salt, and one carrot, an onion and a bouquet garni. When done pour poulette sauce over all.

Sauce poulette. Simmer three shallots in butter, but do not brown. Add one-half glass of white wine and reduce till almost dry. Then add chives sliced fine, sliced French mushrooms, and one pint of sauce Allemande. Boil for a few minutes, and bind with the yolk of an egg and a piece of fresh butter.

Bisque of clams. Simmer one onion, a little celery and leeks, one bay leaf and a few pepper berries in butter. Add the juice of one quart of clams, one pint of fish broth or water, and one cup of rice, and boil for an hour. Strain through a fine sieve, put back on fire and add one pint of cream. When hot add three ounces of butter, salt and a little Cayenne pepper. Parboil the clams, add the juice to the soup, cut the clams in small pieces and serve in the soup terrine. If desired both clams and broth can be used in making the bisque, and all strained before serving.

Tournedos Massenet. Small tenderloin steaks sauté in butter, and seasoned with salt and pepper. Garnish in bouquets with hearts of artichokes cut in four, sliced cèpes, small squares of tomatoes sauté in butter, French fried onions, and Olivette potatoes. Serve with sauce Madère.

Jets de houblons. (Hop sprouts). Can be obtained in cans. Warm in their own juice, drain, serve in vegetable dish, and cover with Hollandaise sauce.

Mince meat. One pound of beef suet chopped fine, one pound of boiled beef cut in very small dices, one pound of seedless raisins, one pound of cleaned currants, one-half pound of seeded Sultana raisins, one-half pound of citron cut in very small dices, one-pound of orange and lemon peel mixed and chopped fine, two pounds of chopped peeled apples, one ounce of ground cinnamon, one ounce of cloves, allspice, ginger and mace mixed, one pint of rum, and one pint of brandy. Mix well, put in jars and keep in cool place. Use as needed.

Mince pie. Line pie plate with dough as for apple pie. Put in mince meat, and finish as for apple pie. Serve warm with a piece of American cheese on the side.

BREAKFAST
  Baked apples
  Baked beans, Boston style
  Boston brown bread
  Coffee

LUNCHEON
  Écrevisse salad, gourmet
  Eggs, Henri IV
  Broiled squab chicken
  Soufflé potatoes
  Apricot compote
  French pastry   Coffee

DINNER
  Lynn Haven oysters on shell
  Chicken okra soup
  Salted Jordan almonds
  Fillet of halibut, Mornay
  Roast ribs of beef
  Stuffed tomatoes, Noyer
  Sweet potatoes, Southern style
  Wine jelly
  Caroline cakes
  Coffee

Stuffed tomatoes, Noyer. Cut the tops off two nice tomatoes, scoop them out and season with salt and pepper. Mix fresh bread crumbs and chopped

English walnuts in equal parts and fill the tomatoes with same. Put a piece of butter on top and bake in moderate oven for ten minutes.

Baked apples. Wash and core the apples. With a sharp knife cut a circle through the skin, around the apple, above the center, to prevent the apples from bursting. Place on a pan and fill the hole in each with sugar mixed with a little ground cinnamon. Put a small piece of butter on top of each, and a little water in the bottom of the pan. Bake in a moderate oven. Serve with their own juice. Cream separate.

Baked beans, Boston style. Soak three pounds of white beans over night in cold water. Then put same in a one and one-half gallon earthern pot with one-half cup of molasses, one soupspoonful of English mustard mixed with a cup of water, a little salt, and one whole piece of fat, parboiled salt pork. Pour in just enough water to moisten, cover, and put in bake oven for four hours. Or in a not too hot range oven for two and one-half hours. If range is used, be careful that they do not burn. Serve from pot, or in small individual pots, with Boston brown bread separate.

Écrevisse salad, gourmet. Cover the bottoms of four dinner plates with chicory salad. In the center make a nest of celery cut in thin strips like matches. On top of that one well-washed fresh mushroom head, cut the same way, and to cap all, put the tails of six écrevisses. Sprinkle with salt and pepper, and a sauce of one-third tarragon vinegar and two-thirds olive oil. Cut two truffles like matches, and with some fine chervil, sprinkle all over the salad.

Eggs Henri IV. Breaded poached eggs fried in swimming lard. Place on a piece of toast spread with purée de foie gras, and cover with sauce Périgordine.

Sauce Périgordine. To one cup of brown gravy add one spoonful of chopped truffles reduced in sherry wine. Season with salt and Cayenne pepper.

Broiled squab chicken. Split a squab from the back, salt, pepper, moisten with a little olive oil and broil. Serve on toast, with maître d'hôtel sauce, quartered lemons and watercress.

BREAKFAST
  Florida grapefruit
  Eggs Bercy
  Rolls
  Coffee

LUNCHEON
  Consommé in cups
  Fried smelts, Tartar sauce
  Broiled pig's feet, special
  Fried apples
  Romaine salad
  French pastry   Coffee

DINNER
  Seapuit oysters
  Potage Lamballe
  Boiled beef garnished with vegetables
  Horseradish à l'Anglaise   Pickles
  Asparagus, Hollandaise
  Fancy ice cream
  Assorted cakes   Coffee

Eggs Bercy. Fry some small breakfast sausages and cut in pieces one inch long. Make some shirred eggs. When half cooked add the sausages and a very little tomato sauce. Season with salt and pepper and finish cooking.

Broiled pig's feet, special. Take some boiled pig's feet, split, and remove the upper bones. Season with salt, pepper and olive oil, roll in fresh bread crumbs, and broil. See sauce below.

Sauce special. Two-thirds tomato ketchup, one-third tomato sauce, a little paprika, a little Worcestershire sauce. Bring to a boil and serve.

Boiled pig's feet. Roll two pig's feet very tightly together with cheesecloth, so they will lay straight when cooked. Put in vessel, cover with cold water, season with salt, whole black peppers, carrot, onion, and a bouquet garni. Boil until well done. If necessary to keep them after cooking, place in an earthern pot in their own broth.

Fried apples. Peel, core, and cut the apples in five or six pieces. Roll in flour and fry in swimming fat or lard. Serve on a napkin.

Icing or frosting, for glacé cakes, éclairs, etc. One and one-half pounds of icing sugar, a pony of water or fruit juice, and the whites of two eggs. Mix and heat over slow fire, stirring continually with a wooden spoon. Do not let it boil. Flavor according to desire. For chocolate frosting add a little melted cocoa.

Cream puffs. One-quarter pound of butter, one cup of water, one cup of milk, four eggs and one-quarter pound of flour. Put the butter, water and milk into a sauce pan and boil. Remove from the fire and add the flour, mixing with a wooden spoon. Then add the eggs one by one, beating well. Dress them on a buttered pan, and about two inches in diameter. Moisten the tops with eggs, and sprinkle with chopped almonds. Bake in a medium oven for about twenty minutes, then slit one edge and fill with sweet whipped cream. Dust some powdered sugar on top and serve.

Chocolate éclairs. Same dough as for cream puffs. Dress them on a buttered pan in the shape of lady fingers, and bake in hot oven. Split at one side and fill with sweet whipped cream. Coat with chocolate icing. Pastry cream may be used instead of whipped cream, if desired.

Pastry cream. Pint of milk, one-half of a vanilla bean, one-quarter pound of sugar, three eggs and one ounce of corn starch. Mix the eggs, sugar and corn starch. Boil the vanilla bean and add to the eggs. Mix well with a whip, put on fire and keep stirring until thick. When cold use it for filling small cakes, cream puffs, éclairs, etc.

BREAKFAST	DINNER
Preserved figs	California oysters on half shell

Wheat cakes
Rolls
Coffee

LUNCHEON

Anchovy salad
Poached eggs, sans gêne
Navarin of lamb, printanier
Baba au rhum
Demi tasse

Purée of lentils
Stuffed roasted chicken
String beans
Duchesse potatoes
Cold French asparagus, French dressing
Almond cake
Coffee

SUPPER

Salade Olga

Wheat cakes. Sift together into a bowl one-half pound of flour and one teaspoonful of baking powder. Add one ounce of sugar, one ounce of melted butter, one egg and a little milk. Mix all into a medium thick batter. Bake on a hot griddle iron. Serve honey or maple syrup, and sweet butter separate.

Breakfast rolls. Three pounds of flour, one ounce of salt, one ounce of sugar and two ounces of yeast. Scald the milk and pour it over the sugar, salt and butter. Melt the yeast in luke-warm water, mix with the milk, etc., and add half of the flour. Beat well, cover, and let raise. Then add the remainder of the flour and let it raise again until it is twice its original volume. Put on table, roll in shape desired, place on pan, and let raise again. Brush the top with melted butter, and bake.

Anchovy salad. Put sliced lettuce on the bottom of a pickle dish. Place fillets of anchovies crosswise over the lettuce. Garnish all around with chopped eggs, beets and parsley. Season with French dressing.

Poached eggs, sans gêne. Place a hot poached egg on a heart of artichoke, cover with a slice of parboiled beef marrow. Serve with sauce Bordelaise.

Navarin of lamb, printanier. (Lamb stew). Take three pounds of shoulder, or breast of lamb, and cut in pieces two inches square. Salt, pepper, and put in sauté pan with a little fat or butter, and allow to roast until nice and brown. Then add a cup of flour and let same become brown. Add a cup of purée of tomatoes and enough hot water to cover the meat, and boil for ten minutes. Parboil three carrots and three turnips and cut in small pieces, and add together with twelve whole small onions fried brown in butter, twelve small round potatoes, and a bouquet garni. Cook until soft, remove the bouquet garni, and serve with chopped parsley and fresh cooked peas on top.

Duchesse potatoes. Make dough as for potato croquettes. Roll on table with a little flour, and cut in the shape of a cork. Flatten and cut a cross on the top with a small knife, brush with yolks of eggs, put on buttered pan and bake in oven. By using a pastry bag with a star mould the tops can be decorated with the dough, in the form of a rose, in place of the cross.

Salade Olga. Cut into small dices two apples, one stalk of celery, two buttons of cooked artichokes, a few asparagus tips, and one truffle. Season with salt, pepper, and a very little vinegar and oil. Place in salad bowl with leaves of lettuce around the sides, and cover with mayonnaise. Garnish with fancy-cut pickled beets and artichokes. Sprinkle with hard-boiled yolks of eggs chopped fine, and parsley.

BREAKFAST
- Oatmeal with cream
- Boiled salt mackerel, melted butter
- Baked potatoes
- Rolls
- Coffee

LUNCHEON
- Stuffed eggs, Nantua
- Mutton chop, grilled
- Saratoga chip potatoes
- Chiffonnade salad
- Camembert cheese
- Coffee

DINNER

Cream of asparagus
Whitebait on Graham bread
Rheinbraten
Romaine salad
Cup custard
Lady fingers
Coffee

Stuffed eggs, Nantua. Cut four hard-boiled eggs in two, lengthwise, and remove the yolks. Mix a piece of butter, the size of an egg, with a little anchovy paste, a very little salt, pepper, paprika, chopped parsley, and the yolks strained through a coarse sieve. Dress or fill the eggs through a pastry bag, put a slice of pimento on top of each, and serve very cold.

Mutton chops, grilled. Salt and pepper the chops, roll in oil and broil. Garnish with watercress.

Saratoga chip potatoes. Round the potatoes off lengthwise to about the size of a silver dollar. Slice very thin, fry in swimming fat until crisp, remove and salt. Serve on napkin. Do not cover or they will become soft.

Chiffonnade salad. Equal parts of romaine, lettuce, chicory, escarole, sliced cucumbers and quartered tomatoes. Put in salad bowl, pour French dressing over all, and garnish with chopped beets, eggs and parsley.

Cream of asparagus. Prepare same as cream of cauliflower. Use either canned or fresh asparagus.

Whitebait on Graham bread. Wash the whitebait and dry, then put in bowl, season with salt and pepper, and cover with milk. Remove and roll in flour, using a colander to allow the flour to sift through. Fry in swimming lard, which is ready in advance, and very hot. Serve on napkin, and garnish with Graham bread and butter sandwiches, fried parsley, quartered lemon, and sauce Tartar separate, or any kind of cold sauce.

Rheinbraten. Cut sirloin steaks one-half inch thick. Season with salt and paprika on both sides, and fry in hot butter. Dish up on platter with paprika sauce, and garnish with paprika potatoes.

Paprika sauce. Simmer one chopped onion and a chopped slice of raw ham, in a little butter. Add one cup of cream, two cups of cream sauce, a soupspoonful of paprika, and a little salt. Boil for ten minutes and strain.

Paprika potatoes. Slice fresh-boiled potatoes and put in sauce pan. Cover with paprika sauce, salt, and boil for a few minutes.

27

BREAKFAST
  Assorted fruits
  Boiled eggs
  Rolls
  Coffee

LUNCHEON
  Cold assorted meats
  Potato salad
  Coffee

DINNER
  Clear green turtle, au Xérès
  Toke Point oysters, mignonette
  Salted almonds   Celery
  Radishes   Ripe olives
  Planked striped bass
  Sweetbread patties, cream sauce
  Roast stuffed turkey, with chestnuts
  Cranberry sauce
  Sweet potatoes, Southern style
  Succotash
  Hearts of lettuce, egg dressing
  Plum pudding, hard and brandy sauces
  Mince pie
  Fancy ice cream

> Assorted cakes
> Roquefort cheese and crackers
> Assorted fruits
> Coffee

Mignonnette sauce. Take one-half cup of whole white peppers and crush with a bottle on a hard table or marble slab, but not too fine. Mix with four finely chopped shallots, a little chives, one spoonful of salt and one-half pint of white wine or tarragon vinegar. Serve in a green pepper, or a small glass, in center of plate surrounded with oysters or clams.

Planked striped bass. Split the bass, remove the bones, place on buttered plank, season with salt, pepper and a little melted butter over all. Bake in oven until nearly done. Take out and decorate with a pastry bag and a star mould, with some potato prepared as for potato croquettes, forming a border around the fish. Put back in oven and bake until nice and brown. Pour maître d'hôtel sauce on top, garnish with quartered lemons and parsley in branches.

Turkey stuffed with chestnuts. Stuff the turkey with chestnut dressing. Put some thin-sliced pork fat over the breast and tie together. Place in pan with an onion, carrot, a little thyme, bay leaf and fresh piece of butter. Salt, put in oven and baste all the time. When turkey is done remove from pan, and let gravy set for a few minutes. Take off the fat, add a little stock or water, reduce one-half, add a little meat extract and strain.

Dressing for chicken, turkey, suckling pig, etc. Bake six onions, with the skins on, in oven for ten minutes. Remove the skins and chop very fine. Add turkey, chicken or suckling pig livers cut in very small squares. Then add fresh bread crumbs, a piece of fresh butter, salt and pepper. Mix well, add a little powdered thyme, chopped parsley, add garlic if desired. If for suckling pig add some sage.

Chestnut dressing. Split the shells of two pounds of chestnuts with a sharp pointed knife. Put in oven and when they burst open remove and peel. Put in pot with a small piece of celery, salt, cover with water, boil till done, allow to cool, and mix with dressing described above.

Apple dressing. Peel half a dozen apples, remove the cores, cut in six pieces, put in pan with three ounces of butter and simmer slowly for ten minutes. Mix with above dressing, omitting chestnuts.

28

BREAKFAST
 Hothouse raspberries with cream
 Oatmeal and cream
 Stewed lamb kidneys
 Rolls
 Coffee

LUNCHEON
 Grapefruit with cherries
 Turkey hash on toast
 Coffee éclairs
 Oolong tea

DINNER
 Consommé aux quenelles
 Ripe California olives
 Cultivated brook trout, Hollandaise
 Potatoes nature
 Roast ribs of prime beef
 Stewed tomatoes
 Mashed potatoes
 Lettuce salad
 English breakfast tea ice cream
 Assorted fancy cakes
 Coffee

SUPPER
 Welsh rabbit

Stewed lamb kidneys. Split six kidneys, remove the skin, and cut in thin slices. Have a pan ready with hot butter and fry on a quick fire for a few seconds. Take kidneys from pan, and add one soupspoonful of flour to the sauce and let simmer until brown. Add one cup of stock or hot water, salt and pepper, and reduce one-half. Return the kidneys to the sauce, but do not let them boil or they will become hard. Before serving add a little sherry wine or chopped parsley.

Turkey hash on toast. Cut turkey in small dices, put in sauce pan, cover with two-thirds boiling cream and one-third cream sauce, season, boil for a few minutes, and serve on hot dry toast.

Welsh rabbit. Cut one pound of American cheese in very small dices. Put in pan with a small pinch of Cayenne pepper, one spoonful of ale or beer, one teaspoonful of Worcestershire sauce, and put on fire to melt. Do not stir until cheese is quite soft; then stir well with whip till it is melted and boiling. Pour over toast on a very hot china platter or shirred egg dish.

French bread. One gallon of warm water, two ounces of yeast, three ounces of salt, three ounces of sugar and three ounces of lard. Dissolve the yeast, salt, sugar and lard in the water, and mix in flour enough to form a medium-stiff dough. Work it until smooth, cover with a cloth and let it raise for one-half hour. Then form the dough into long loaves and about two inches thick. Lay them on a cloth dusted with flour and let them raise to nearly double in size. Moisten the tops with milk, make several diagonal cuts on each loaf half way through, and bake in a rather hot oven.

Homemade bread. One quart of warm water, one quart of warm milk, two ounces of yeast, one ounce of salt and one-quarter of a pound of melted lard or butter. Dissolve the yeast in the milk and butter, and add the salt and butter, or lard. Add enough flour to make a medium dough, mix, beat well and cover. Allow to raise for about four hours. Divide the dough in four parts, roll and place in moulds or pans and let raise another hour before baking.

Orange juice
Scrambled eggs with anchovies
Rolls
Coffee

Écrevisses with mayonnaise

Lamb chops sauté, aux cèpes

Sybil potatoes

Cup custard

Coffee

DINNER

Toke Point oysters on half shell

Cream of summer squash

Filet mignon, Chéron

Georgette potatoes

Ravachol salad

Pistache ice cream

Baked Alaska

Coffee

Scrambled eggs with anchovies. Put some fillets of salted anchovies in oil and leave for a few days; or use anchovies in oil. Salt the scrambled eggs lightly and lay the anchovies crosswise over the top.

Écrevisses with mayonnaise. Prepare the écrevisses en buisson. When cold remove the tails from the shells and serve on platter with lemons and parsley. Mayonnaise separate.

Lamb chops sauté, aux cèpes. Fry the chops in sauté pan, in oil. When done put on platter. Slice some cèpes, (a specie of mushroom) season with salt and pepper and fry for a few seconds. Just before removing from the fire add a little garlic, and pour all over the chops. Sprinkle with chopped parsley.

Georgette potatoes. Use potato croquette dough. Roll on table to the thickness of a cork and about ten inches long. Make a hollow the entire length and fill with purée of spinach. Bring the edges of the hollow together and roll again so the spinach will be in the middle of the potato dough and not visible. Cut in pieces two inches long, roll in bread crumbs, and fry in the same manner as croquettes.

Ravachol salad. Use whole leaves of romaine. Place alternate slices of grape fruit and orange on top until the leaves are covered. Put some narrow strips of red pepper across the top, pour French dressing over all, and decorate with unsweetened whipped cream.

Filet mignon, Chéron. Small fillets of beef sauté in butter. Cover with Béarnaise sauce, and garnish with artichoke buttons, macédoine, (mixed vegetables) and fleurons.

Fleurons. Used for garnishing entrées, Newburg or chafing dish preparations, fish, etc. Take some puff paste, with six turns, roll it to about one-eighth inch in thickness, cut with a half moon cutter about two inches in diameter, and place on a pan moistened with water. Wash the tops with eggs and bake in a hot oven.

30

BREAKFAST
- Hominy and cream
- Calf's liver and bacon
- Baked potatoes
- Rolls
- Coffee

LUNCHEON
- Stuffed tomatoes, Nana
- Poached eggs, Persanne
- Broiled squab on toast
- Cold asparagus, mustard sauce
- Saratoga chip potatoes
- German apple cake
- Coffee

DINNER
- Onion soup, au gratin
- Celery
- Planked striped bass
- Roast leg of veal, au jus
- Cardon à la moelle
- Potatoes à la Reine
- Escarole and chicory salad
- Neapolitan ice cream
- Assorted cakes
- Coffee

Stuffed tomatoes, Nana. Put four nice medium sized tomatoes in boiling water for fifteen seconds. Then dip in cold water and peel. Cut off the tops, scoop out and fill with the following: One-half of the breast of a boiled chicken, chopped very fine, some chopped walnuts, a little mayonnaise sauce, a little whipped cream, and salt and pepper. Mix well. After filling place the tomatoes on lettuce leaves and cover with thin mayonnaise. Serve very cold.

Calf's liver and bacon. Slice the liver about two-thirds of an inch thick. Salt, pepper, pass through olive oil and broil, but not too well done or the liver will be hard. Serve broiled bacon on top, maître d'hôtel sauce, and garnish with lemon and parsley.

Mustard sauce, cold. For asparagus, artichokes, etc. To one cup of mayonnaise sauce add one soupspoonful of French mustard. Mix well.

Lunch rolls. Two pounds of flour, one ounce of yeast, one ounce of salt, one pint of water. Dissolve the yeast and salt in the water, add the flour and mix, making a rather hard dough. Put into a basin, cover with a cloth, and allow to stand for four hours. Then divide the dough in four parts, roll each one separately into the form of a stick about fourteen inches long and one inch thick. Put on a cloth on a special roll plank made for the purpose. Take care that the rolls are sufficiently far apart so they will not touch when they raise. Let them set for about one-half hour. Then cut each roll of dough in three parts with a sharp knife, make two incisions in the top of each, put into a pan and bake for about twenty minutes.

Cardons à la moelle. Cardon is a vegetable, a thistle-like plant related to the artichoke. It can be obtained in cans. Empty into a vessel and warm in its own juice. Parboil some sliced beef marrow, put into a brown gravy with the juice of one lemon and some chopped parsley. Remove cardon from its broth, put on a platter and pour the brown sauce and marrow over all.

BREAKFAST	LUNCHEON
Preserved figs with cream	Cold fillet of sole, Raven

Force with cream
Dry toast
Coffee

Spring lamb Irish stew
Cream puffs
Coffee

DINNER

Consommé Sévigné
Salted Brazil nuts
Sweetbreads braisé, Pompadour
Château potatoes
Terrine de foie gras à la gelée
Hearts of romaine, Roquefort dressing
Meringue à la crème, Chantilly
Coffee

Cold fillet of sole, Raven. Cook four fillets of sole in white wine and place on a platter. Simmer two spoonsful of finely chopped shallots in butter, add a few chopped fresh mushrooms, one chopped tomato and the wine used for cooking the fish. Reduce until it becomes thick, cool off, add some chives and chervil chopped fine, and a little mayonnaise. Spread over the fillets, and cover with a mayonnaise rose. Decorate to taste with fancy-cut truffles, pickles, etc. Serve very cold.

Consommé Sévigné. White meat of chicken and smoked beef tongue cut Julienne, (in the shape of matches). Serve in consommé with a sprinkle of chopped chervil.

Sweetbreads braisé, Pompadour. Braise the sweetbreads until about two-thirds done. Cool a little and cover with a thin layer of chicken force meat. Decorate all around with chopped tongue, with chopped truffles in the center. Replace in pan, using the same stock used before, but strained. Cover with buttered manilla paper and return to oven to finish cooking. Serve with own gravy and a little Madeira sauce.

Terrine de foie gras à la gelée. Put the foie gras on ice for a few hours. Carve from the terrine with a table spoon and place on a platter covered with a napkin. Decorate with meat jelly cut in triangles and chopped, and parsley in branches.

Gelée. (Meat jelly). Take any kind of good stock. Put in the whites of six eggs to each gallon to clarify it. Add one pound of chopped raw beef to the gallon. Also one sliced onion, one carrot, one leek, a little celery and parsley, a few pepper berries, one bay leaf and a clove. Stir well and add slowly the hot stock. Soak twelve leaves of gelatine in cold water for ten minutes and add. Bring to a boil slowly, stirring from time to time. When it comes to a boil it must be clear. Strain through very fine cheese cloth, being careful not to stir up the meat so that it will cloud the broth. Season with salt and a very little Cayenne, add a glass of good sherry, and allow to cool.

Meringue à la crème, Chantilly. Whip some cream until stiff, add some powdered sugar, flavor with vanilla. Put one spoonful between each two meringue shells, dress on a plate, and decorate with some of the same cream passed through a pastry bag with a star mould.

2

BREAKFAST
  Baked apples
  Oatmeal with cream
  Butter toast
  Coffee

LUNCHEON
  Eggs, Tivoli
  Miroton of beef, en bordure
  Cabinet pudding
  Coffee

DINNER
  Blue Point oysters
  Consommé Doria
  Fillet of sole, St. Malo
  Tournedos, Boulanger
  Soufflé potatoes
  Roquefort cheese
  Crackers

Coffee

Eggs, Tivoli. Cut a piece of homemade bread into a cube and fry in butter. Open one side with a sharp knife and scoop out the center. Place in the cavity a poached egg, cover with cream sauce, sprinkle a little grated cheese on top, and bake until brown.

Miroton of beef, en bordure. Use left over boiled or braised beef, and cut in thin slices. Put into sauce pan one sliced onion with a piece of butter, and simmer until nice and brown. Then add one gill of vinegar, and a spoonful of French mustard and reduce until almost dry. Now add the sliced beef, cover with brown gravy, season with salt, pepper and a little chopped parsley, and boil for a few minutes. Dish into a deep platter, or individual shirred egg dishes, make a border of potato croquet dough, sprinkle grated cheese on top and bake till brown.

Consommé Doria. Consommé tapioca, with chopped truffles and sherry wine.

Fillet of sole, St. Malo. Fillet of sole au vin blanc with the addition of lobster sauce with scallops, and lobster and oysters cut in small squares.

Tournedos, Boulanger. Small fillets of beef sauté, with sauce Madère. Garnished with fried calf's brains and artichoke bottoms stuffed with spinach.

Soufflé potatoes. Peel the potatoes to oval shape. Do not wash but wipe with a napkin. Cut lengthwise in strips about an eighth of an inch in thickness. Place in swimming fat or lard that is merely warm and put on fire to get hot. When the potatoes are nearly done they will swim on top of the fat and swell up like little cushions. When all are on top take out and throw into very hot fat to color them. Remove, salt, and serve on napkin.

BREAKFAST
  Baked apples
  Oatmeal with cream
  Butter toast
  Coffee

LUNCHEON
  Eggs, Tivoli
  Miroton of beef, en bordure
  Cabinet pudding
  Coffee

DINNER
  Hors d'oeuvre variés
  Cream of squash
  Aiguillettes of bass, à la Russe
  Squab sauté, Tyrolienne
  Anna potatoes
  Strawberry ice cream
  Assorted cakes
  Coffee

Corn Muffins. One-half pound of corn meal, one-half pound of flour, two ounces of melted butter, four eggs, one pint of sour milk, one-half cup of molasses, one teaspoonful of soda and one teaspoonful of salt. Sift together the corn meal, flour and salt. Dissolve the soda in the sour milk, add the eggs, well beaten, the molasses, the butter and the sifted ingredients. Beat well and bake in a well-greased muffin pan.

Eggs en Cocotte, Italienne. Put in buttered cocotte dish one raw egg, cover with sauce Italienne, put a little grated cheese and a small piece of butter on top and bake in oven.

Italienne sauce. Chop six shallots very fine and simmer in sauce pan with two ounces of butter. Do not let the shallots become brown or they will lose their flavor. Add some chopped fresh or canned mushrooms (about a can full), and one glass of white wine, and boil until reduced almost dry. Then add one and one-half pints of brown gravy, and boil again for a few minutes. Season with salt and pepper to taste, and sprinkle with chopped parsley. This sauce is used for many entrée dishes.

Endive salad. Endive is a species of chicory salad, originally imported from France. Cut in two lengthwise and lay on platter or individual plates.

Serve with a sauce of salt, pepper, and one-fourth tarragon vinegar to three-fourths olive oil. Sprinkle with chopped chervil.

Chicken hash, Victor. Take the white meat of a boiled chicken or soup hen and cut in half inch squares, and half as much fresh-boiled potatoes cut the same way. Chop six shallots very fine and simmer in four ounces of sweet butter, but do not let them become colored. Add the chicken and potatoes, and cover with clear chicken broth. Season with salt, pepper and a little chives, and let simmer for five minutes. Serve in a chafing dish with a sprinkle of chopped chervil on top. Melba toast separate.

4

BREAKFAST
- Grapefruit juice
- Shredded wheat biscuit with cream
- English muffins
- Coffee

LUNCHEON
- Casaba melon
- Eggs aromatic
- English lamb chops, XX Century Club
- Lettuce salad
- Pistache éclairs
- Coffee

DINNER
- Blue Point oysters
- Fillet of bass, shrimp sauce
- Braised beef, Cumberland style
- Baked Hubbard squash
- Mashed potatoes
- Endive salad
- Vanilla ice cream
- Assorted cakes

Coffee

Eggs aromatic. Fry the eggs in oil or poach. Place on toast, cover with tomato sauce, and put a few leaves of fresh mint on top before serving.

English lamb chops, XX Century Club. Broil the chops, garnish with pimentos stuffed with purée of sweet potatoes. Serve with sauce Madère.

Pistache Éclairs. Same as chocolate éclairs. Cover with pistache icing.

Pistache icing. To white icing add some pistache essence, or orange flower extract, and a little green coloring.

Fillet of bass, shrimp sauce. Place the fillets in a buttered pan, season with salt, add one-half glass of white wine, and a little stock or water. When cooked dish up on platter and cover with shrimp sauce.

Shrimp sauce. To some white wine sauce (sauce vin blanc) add some shrimps.

Braised beef with calf's feet. Take a piece of round or rump of beef, season with salt and pepper, put in pot with two onions cut in four, two carrots and a piece of butter. Roast until nice and brown. Then add one spoonful of flour and brown again. Add one glass of claret, one quart of stock, three tomatoes cut in four, or canned tomatoes, and a bouquet garni. Bring to a boil, cover tight and put in oven till very well done. This is braised beef, plain. When served Cumberland style (with calf's feet) add the feet at the same time as the claret and stock, and strain the sauce when done. If the feet are not served with the beef they may be used as an entrée.

Baked Hubbard squash. Cut the squash in four, remove the seeds, salt and pepper, put a piece of butter on top of each piece of squash and bake in oven.

BREAKFAST
  Sliced oranges
  Boiled salt mackerel
  Baked potatoes
  Corn bread
  Coffee

LUNCHEON
  Clam broth in cups
  Ripe olives
  Fillet of turbot, Pelissier
  Potatoes Parisienne
  Spinach aux croutons
  Omelette au rhum
  Coffee

DINNER
  Lobster chowder
  Celery   Salted English walnuts
  Aiguillettes of sole, Venitienne
  Planked striped bass
  Cucumber salad
  Brussels sprouts and chestnuts
  Apple Charlotte
  Coffee

Clam broth. Take hard or soft clams and wash well. Put in vessel with just water enough to cover, a little salt and a small piece of raw celery. Boil for fifteen minutes, and strain through cheese cloth.

Clam broth, Chantilly. Serve whipped cream separate, or on top of each cup.

Consommé en Bellevue. Half chicken broth and half clam broth mixed. Serve in cups with whipped cream on top.

Clam chowder. Chop two onions, one leek, a piece of celery and one green onion in small pieces, also cut one-half pound of salt pork in small squares. Put all together in a vessel with two ounces of butter and simmer till well done. Then add one gallon of stock or fish broth, four potatoes cut in half inch squares, salt, pepper, a little paprika, one teaspoonful of sugar, one teaspoonful of chopped thyme, a little chopped parsley, and four peeled tomatoes cut in small dices; or chopped canned tomatoes. Bring to a boil and let cook for about one hour. Put one hundred well-washed Little Neck clams in a separate vessel and put on fire with one-half glass of water and boil for ten minutes. Strain the broth and add to the chowder. Remove the clams from the shells, cut in four pieces and add to the chowder with one cup of cracker meal, and boil for four minutes. Serve with broken crackers.

Lobster chowder. Same as clam chowder with the exception of lobster cut in small dices instead of the clams.

6

BREAKFAST
- Bananas with cream
- Boiled eggs
- Dry toast
- Chocolate
- Whipped cream

LUNCHEON
- Fish salad, ravigote
- Broiled lamb chops
- French fried potatoes
- Cauliflower Polonaise
- German coffee cake
- Lunch rolls
- Tea

DINNER
- Cream of endives
- Fillet of flounder, Chevreuse
- Chicken sauté, Ambassadrice
- Carrots, Vichy
- Fondante potatoes
- Escarole salad
- Peach ice cream

SUPPER
- Oysters poulette
- St. Francis rolls
- Nesselrode pudding
- Lady fingers
- Demi tasse

Assorted cakes

Coffee

Oysters poulette. Open three dozen oysters, put in vessel with their own juice and bring to a boil. Drain off the broth, cover oysters with a pint of poulette sauce, and serve in chafing dish.

Carrots, Vichy. Slice some tender carrots very fine, place in buttered sauce pan, season with salt and a little pepper, and simmer over a slow fire. Then add a little chicken broth or soup stock and cook until soft. Mix one teaspoonful of flour with three ounces of butter, add to the carrots and simmer for five minutes. Serve with chopped parsley.

Chocolate. For each person take one rib or bar of chocolate. Cut in very small pieces, put in pot and add one spoonful of water and let chocolate melt. Add one large cup of very hot milk for each person, and bring nearly to the boiling point.

Fish salad, ravigote. Any kind of boiled fish that may be left over. Remove the bones and skin, break the fish in small pieces and lay on lettuce leaves. Cover with Tartar sauce, garnish with sliced pickles, pickled beets and hard-boiled eggs.

Cream of endives. Prepare the same as cream of cauliflower, using endives instead.

Fillet of flounder, Chevreuse. Stuff the fillets with halibut force meat, put in buttered pan and cook in white wine. Cover with Béarnaise sauce mixed with a little purée of tomatoes.

Chicken sauté, Ambassadrice. Jointed chicken sauté in butter, sauce suprême, garnished with truffles, mushrooms and goose liver sauté.

Goose liver sauté. Salt and pepper some fresh goose livers, roll in flour, put in pan with fresh butter and simmer until done. For garnishing entrée dishes the imported goose liver au natural can be obtained in cans. Remove the fat from the top of the can, cut the liver out in slices, season with salt and pepper, put in flour, and fry very quickly in sweet butter. Serve as a garnish or as an entrée.

Goose liver sauté aux truffes. Put goose liver sauté in chafing dish and cover with sauce Périgord.

Sauce Périgord. Slice six truffles very thin, put in vessel with a glass of dry sherry wine and reduce until it is nearly dry. Then add one-half pint of brown gravy, seasoned with salt and Cayenne pepper, and cook for ten minutes.

7

BREAKFAST
- Oatmeal with cream
- Baked beans, Boston style
- Boston brown bread
- Coffee

LUNCHEON
- Mariniert herring
- Boiled potatoes
- Rolls
- Coffee

DINNER
- Chicken okra soup
- Salted pecans
- Fillet of sole, Normande
- Roast ribs of beef
- Asparagus, Hollandaise
- Brabant potatoes
- Bijou salad
- Hazelnut ice cream
- Alsatian wafers
- Coffee

Corn bread. One-half pound of yellow corn meal, one-half pound of flour, one teaspoonful of baking powder, three eggs, one ounce of melted butter, one teaspoonful of salt, one pint of milk and one-half cup of boiling water. Pour the boiling water over the corn meal and allow it to become cold. Beat the yolks of the eggs and add to the corn meal, then add the milk, flour and the baking powder, salt and melted butter. Mix and then add the whites of the eggs beaten very stiff. Pour into a shallow well-greased pan and bake in a hot oven for about twenty-five minutes.

Boston brown bread. One pound of rye flour, one pound of Graham flour, two pounds of corn meal, one pound of wheat flour, one quart of molasses, one and one-half quarts of milk, two ounces of salt and three ounces of baking powder. Put all the flour and the baking powder in one vessel, then add the molasses, milk and salt and make a soft dough. Fill brown bread moulds about three-fourths full, put in steam cooker for three and one-half hours, then remove from steam and bake in oven for twenty minutes.

Chicken okra soup. Remove the breast from a raw fowl, and with the remainder make a chicken broth. Cut the breast in small dices, put in vessel with a chopped onion and a chopped green pepper and a small piece of butter, simmer till onion is soft, then add the chicken broth, two peeled tomatoes cut in small dices, or some canned tomatoes, salt and pepper. Let boil slowly for one-half hour, then add one pound of okra cut in pieces three-quarters of an inch in length, and cook until okra is soft. Add one teaspoonful of Worcestershire sauce and a cup of boiled rice and serve with chopped parsley. If desired a slice of ham may be cut in small squares and added at the same time as the chicken breast.

BREAKFAST	LUNCHEON
Stewed prunes	Hors d'oeuvres variés
Scrambled eggs with asparagus tips	Eggs Boremis
Buttered toast	Hungarian beef goulash

Coffee   Apple pie
                                          Coffee

                    DINNER
                      Cream of spinach
                      Fillet of bass, Dieppoise
                      Chicken sauté, Marengo
                      Potatoes à la Reine
                      Dandelion salad
                      Apricot ice cream
                      Macaroons
                      Coffee

Scrambled eggs with asparagus tips. Put some asparagus tips in butter, season with salt and pepper, simmer till hot, and add to the eggs.

Eggs Boremis. Put an egg in a well-buttered cocotte dish, season with salt and pepper, put plenty of grated cheese and a piece of butter on top of all, and bake in oven.

Cocoa. Put two tablespoonsful of cocoa in a pot with one-half cup of water and boil for a minute. Add two cups of milk, bring to a boil, and strain. Serve powdered sugar separate. May also be made with water only, omitting the milk.

Fillet of bass, Dieppoise. Cook the fillets "au vin blanc." Dish up on platter with lobster sauce and oysters, mushrooms, truffles, shrimps and mussels cut in small squares.

Chicken sauté, Marengo. Joint of chicken, season with salt and pepper and put in pan in very hot olive oil. When nice and brown on both sides add four chopped shallots and a little garlic and allow them to get hot, but not brown. Then add one-half glass of white wine and reduce. Add one cup of brown gravy, one cup of chopped tomatoes and one can of French mushrooms. Cook for fifteen minutes. Dish up and garnish with eggs and croûtons fried in oil, chopped parsley, and a few slices of truffle on top.

Pie paste. One and one-half pounds of flour, one-half pound of lard, one-half pound of butter and a pinch of salt. Mix all together and add enough water, (about one cup), to make a rather stiff dough. Keep in cool place or ice box.

Apple pie. For two pies line the plates with pie paste rolled very thin. Slice six good sized apples, add one-quarter of a pound of sugar and a teaspoonful of powdered cinnamon, mix and fill the plates. Wet the edges of the dough and cover with paste also rolled thin. Wash over with egg, make a few cuts in the center so the steam may escape while baking, and put in a moderate oven. When done dust with powdered sugar, and serve hot or cold as desired. If the apples are coarse it will be well to boil them a little in water with a piece of cinnamon and a very little sugar.

9

BREAKFAST
- Baked apples with cream
- Hominy with cream
- Rolls
- Coffee

LUNCHEON
- Grapefruit en suprême
- Eggs Benedict
- Lamb hash
- Chocolate layer cake
- Coffee

DINNER
- Potage Coulis
- Salted pecans
- Fillet of turbot, Royaldi
- Chicken, Edward VII
- Potato croquettes
- Chiffonnade salad

Parfait au chocolate
Assorted cakes
Coffee

Grapefruit en suprême. Serve in a long-stemmed double grapefruit glass, put shaved ice in large glass around the smaller one. In small glass put sliced grapefruit mixed with powdered sugar. Tie a ribbon, with neat bow, around the glass.

Eggs Benedict. Split an English muffin, toast on the inside, place on each half a small slice of broiled ham, on the ham a poached egg, cover with Hollandaise sauce, and place a piece of truffle on top.

Layer cake. Eight eggs, one-half pound of sugar, one-half pound of flour, one-quarter pound of melted butter, and some flavoring extract. Beat the eggs with the sugar, on slow fire until warm, remove and continue beating until cold. Mix the flour in lightly and then add the melted butter, little by little, and the flavoring. Do not mix too much. Pour into a well-buttered mould and bake in a moderate oven for about three-quarters of an hour. Allow to cool, cut in three or four slices, and fill with cream, or jelly, or marmalade, as desired. Glacé the top with icing and decorate. The American style layer cake is mixed in the same manner, but baked in shallow moulds, requiring only about ten minutes in the oven. The filling is then placed between the cakes, instead of slicing.

Chocolate layer cake. Bake some layers as for moka cake, and put three or four, one on top of another, with chocolate butter cream filling between. The filling is made in the same manner as moka filling, but use one ounce of melted chocolate or cocoa instead of the coffee flavor. Glacé the top of the cake with chocolate frosting and decorate with some of the chocolate cream filling, using pastry bag with fancy tube.

Chicken, Edward VII. Boil the chicken in stock and stuff with rice as for Chicken Diva. Add small squares of truffles and goose liver natural. Serve with curry sauce.

BREAKFAST
- Stewed rhubarb
- Boiled eggs
- Dry toast
- Coffee

LUNCHEON
- Canapé Riga
- Eggs Coquelicot
- Tripe and oysters in cream
- Camembert cheese
- Crackers
- Coffee

DINNER
- Potage Hollandaise
- Stuffed fillet of sole, Diplomate
- Tournedos de Goncourt
- String beans, aux fines herbes
- Julienne potatoes
- Salade Brésilienne
- Floating island
- Pound cake
- Coffee

Eggs Coquelicot. Line a timbale mould with a whole red pepper, (canned pimento) and break an egg into it, season with salt and pepper, and put timbale in a pan in boiling water, and place in oven until egg is cooked. Put some chicken hash in cream on a platter and turn egg and pepper on top to look like a little red cap. Serve with cream sauce around the hash.

Tripe and oysters in cream. Simmer six chopped shallots in butter, but do not allow them to color. Add two pounds of tripe cut in strips, one cup of stock, one bouquet garni, and boil for one hour. Remove the bouquet garni, drain off the broth. Add two cups of cream sauce and three dozen parboiled oysters. Simmer for a minute, and season with salt and a little Cayenne pepper.

Potage Hollandaise. (Soup). Bind a velouté of chicken with cream and yolks of eggs. Serve with brunoise garnishing.

Velouté. Used for the foundation of many soups. Put in vessel five ounces of butter and four ounces of flour and simmer for a few minutes. Add two quarts of chicken broth, stock or bouillon, cook for half an hour and bind with one cup of cream and the yolks of two eggs.

Consommé brunoise. Cut in very small dice, (nearly fine chopped), one carrot, one turnip, one leek, a stalk of celery and a little white cabbage, and parboil in salt water. Then drain off the water, put in well-buttered casserole, add a pinch of sugar, cover with buttered manilla paper and with the casserole cover on top of that, and put in the oven to braise. If too dry a half cup of stock may be added. Cook until vegetables are soft. Use for potage garnishing, Consommé brunoise, and other dishes. For soups use one heaping spoonful of brunoise to each plate.

Fillet of sole, Diplomate. Slice fine six fresh mushrooms, season with salt and pepper, and simmer in butter. When done add one spoonful of meat extract. Split four fillets of sole and fill with the above dressing and cook "au vin blanc." Then place on a platter, cover with cream sauce well seasoned, put grated cheese on top and bake in oven.

Tournedos de Goncourt. Broiled fillet of beef served with Béarnaise sauce mixed with a little purée of tomatoes, and garnished with tomatoes glacées.

Tomatoes glacées. Put six whole peeled tomatoes on a buttered pan, season with salt and pepper, put a small piece of butter on top of each, and bake in moderate oven for ten minutes.

BREAKFAST
  Grapefruit juice
  Omelet with ham
  Puff paste crescents

LUNCHEON
  Canapé Martha
  Cold assorted meats
  Potato salad

Oolong tea

Cherry tartelettes

Coffee

DINNER

Blue Points
Consommé brunoise
Braised salmon, Parisienne
Boiled leg of mutton, caper sauce
Mashed turnips
Roast chicken
Hearts of lettuce salad
Biscuit glacé
Assorted cakes
Coffee

Omelet with ham. Cut a slice of cooked ham in small squares, put in omelet pan with a small piece of butter. When hot add three beaten eggs and follow directions for plain omelet, but use a little less salt.

Canapé Martha. Cut a round piece of toast and put some lobster croquette farcé on top in the shape of a pyramid. Put a thin slice of Swiss cheese on top and bake in oven. Garnish with lemon and parsley.

Cherry tartelette. Line tartelette moulds and follow directions as for pear tartelettes, but fill with canned cherries.

Braised salmon, Parisienne. Put a slice of salmon in buttered pan, season with salt and pepper, sprinkle with chopped shallots and parsley, add one one-half glass of white wine, cover and simmer until cooked. Remove fish to platter, and in the pan pour some white wine sauce, (sauce au vin blanc). Let boil for five minutes and pour over fish. Don't strain.

Boiled leg of mutton, caper sauce. Put the leg of mutton in pot and cover with boiling water. Add one carrot, a leek, onion, a little celery and a bouquet garni. Season with salt, and boil for about forty-five minutes.

Caper sauce. Melt three ounces of butter in sauce pan, add three ounces of flour and allow to become hot. Add three pints of stock, bouillon, or the stock from the leg of mutton. Boil for ten minutes, season to taste, bind with the yolk of one egg and a piece of butter, strain, and add one-half cup of capers.

Mashed turnips. Boil or steam a half dozen white or Russian (yellow) turnips. Strain through a fine sieve or colander, add salt and pepper and three ounces of butter. A potato boiled with the turnips will reduce the strong turnip odor.

12

BREAKFAST
- Stewed prunes
- Codfish balls
- Rolls
- Coffee

LUNCHEON
- Oyster broth
- Chow chow
- Bouillabaisse Marseillaise
- Asparagus Hollandaise
- Omelette au confiture
- Coffee

DINNER
- Clam chowder
- Celery
- Oysters à la Hyde
- Striped bass, meunière
- Potatoes nature
- Combination salad
- Fancy ice cream
- Alsatian wafers
- Coffee

Codfish balls. Soak one pound of salt codfish in cold water over night. Then boil in fresh water for ten minutes. Boil two potatoes in salt water and strain through colander or sieve. Shred the codfish very fine and mix with the potato and the yolks of three eggs working well together. Allow to become cool, form into balls, roll in flour and fry in melted butter until nice and golden yellow. Serve on napkins with quartered lemons and parsley in branches.

Bouillabaisse Marseillaise. (Fish stew). Simmer in shallow sauté pan six chopped shallots, one-half onion sliced very fine and one stalk of white leek also finely sliced, in two spoonsful of olive oil, for about one minute. Then add a clove of chopped garlic, one glass of white wine, one pint of fish stock or hot water, salt, pepper, a little Cayenne, a bouquet garni and the tail of a live lobster cut in six slices, and one dozen of well washed Little Neck clams shell and all, boil for ten minutes. Add some solid meat of white fish such as rock cod, bass, tomcods, etc., and a pinch of whole saffron tied in a cloth. Boil again for twenty-five minutes. Do not skim. Remove the saffron and serve in deep dish with the broth. Sprinkle some chopped parsley over the top. Serve separate, slices of bread fried in oil and then rubbed with garlic.

Omelette au confiture. (Jelly omelet). Same as strawberry omelet. Put currant jelly or any kind of marmalade in center of omelet before turning over on platter.

Oysters à la Hyde. Parboil one-half cup of white celery chopped fine, for ten minutes, and allow to cool. Put in sauce pan two dozen large raw oysters with their own juice, add two tablespoonsful of cracker meal, two ounces of butter, one cup of cream and the parboiled celery. Season with salt, pepper, a little Cayenne, and boil for two minutes. If the sauce is not sufficiently thick add a little more cracker meal. Serve in chafing dish.

BREAKFAST
  Griddle cakes
  Honey
  Breakfast sausage
  Rolls
  Coffee

DINNER
  Little Neck clams
  Potage Mongol
  Fillet of sole, Joinville
  Chicken sauté, Bordelaise
  Artichokes Hollandaise
  Potatoes Laurette
  Biscuit Tortoni
  Macaroons
  Coffee

LUNCHEON
  Casaba melon
  Consommé Ditalini
  Eggs Créole
  Stuffed lamb chops, Soubise
  Champs Elysées potatoes
  Romaine salad
  Napoleon cake
  Coffee

SUPPER
  Oysters mignonette
  Salted almonds
  Sweetbreads à la King
  Parfait Napolitain
  Cakes
  Demi tasse

Breakfast sausages. Small pork sausages fried in pan with a small piece of butter. Serve on platter with their own fat.

Consommé Ditalini. Boil some Ditalini (a species of Italian paste), in salt water, drain off and serve in consommé. Grated cheese separate.

Eggs Créole. Put in buttered shirred egg dish one spoonful of Créole sauce, break two eggs in center, and bake in oven.

Créole sauce. Put in sauce pan three ounces of butter, one sliced onion, and three sliced green peppers. Simmer for ten minutes, or until soft, then add one quart of canned tomatoes with their juice, one can of sliced French mushrooms, one-half can of sliced pimentos, a very little finely chopped garlic, and salt and pepper. Cook slowly for one hour. Fresh tomatoes may be substituted for canned, if desired; and if the sauce is too thick some brown gravy or bouillon may be added.

Fillet of sole, Joinville. Cook the fillets "au vin blanc." Serve crayfish sauce or écrevisse, or shrimp sauce with sliced French mushrooms, truffles and lobster.

Potage Mongol. One-third purée of peas, one-third consommé Julienne, one-third purée of tomatoes. Well mixed.

Chicken sauté, Bordelaise. Jointed chicken sauté in butter with a shallot. Serve brown gravy with mushrooms and cèpes sauté, and garnish with fried onions.

Cèpes sauté. Cèpes are a species of mushrooms and may be obtained in cans. Slice and fry in butter and olive oil in equal parts, season with salt and pepper, and when nearly golden yellow add a very finely chopped shallot and some chopped parsley, and simmer for a minute longer. Often used for garnishing entrées, etc.

Fried onions. Cut large onions in thin slices and separate into rings. Put in milk, then in flour, and fry in hot swimming lard. When brown remove, salt, and serve on napkin, or use for garnishing.

BREAKFAST
  Preserved figs
  Oatmeal with cream
  Chickens' livers sauté, au Madère
  Rolls
  Coffee

LUNCHEON
  Cold assorted meats
  Alligator pear, French dressing
  Roquefort cheese
  Crackers
  Coffee

DINNER
  Lynnhaven oysters
  Purée of Lima beans, aux croutons

        Ripe olives
        Sand dabs, meunière
        Louisiana gumbo filé
        Boiled rice
        Russian salad
        Peach Melba
        Assorted cakes
        Coffee

Chickens' livers sauté, au Madère. Cut the livers in three, salt and pepper and fry in sauté pan in butter. Drain off and add a cup of sauce Madère. Do not let them boil in the sauce.

Purée of Lima beans. Take a can of Lima beans, or a quart of fresh beans, put in vessel, cover with chicken broth or bouillon and boil till done. Then strain through fine sieve, put back in vessel, add two ounces of sweet butter, and season to taste. Serve with small squares of bread fried in butter.

Louisiana gumbo filé. Two chickens, one quart of large oysters, one quart of cooked shrimps, six bell peppers, four large onions, one quart of tomatoes, one-half pound of butter, two bunches of celery, one small bunch of parsley, one-quarter teaspoonful of tobasco sauce, and black pepper and salt to suit.

First.—Cut the chicken the same way as for fricassée, and wipe dry.

Second.—Cut onions and brown in butter, and strain.

Third.—Fry chicken brown in strained butter, then set to one side.

Fourth.—Add two tablespoonsful of flour to strained butter and brown gradually. When a rich brown add two quarts of boiling water, then add the tomatoes. Now bring to boiling point and strain through a fine strainer.

Fifth.—Place strained liquor in a large stew pan and add one teaspoonful of salt and a half teaspoonful of black pepper, then add the chicken. Should the liquor not sufficiently cover the chicken add more hot water to about two inches above. Then add the bell peppers and celery without cutting up. Boil over slow fire until chicken can be picked off the bones with fork. Then remove chicken and strip meat from bones and cut in small pieces, remove the celery and bell peppers, and replace chicken. Add the shrimps, oysters and tobasco sauce. Boil for ten minutes. Then gradually add sufficient "filé powder" to bring to a rich creamy consistency. Add to each plate two large tablespoonsful of boiled rice. Serve immediately.

Boiled rice. Wash one-half pound of rice and soak in cold water for an hour. Cook over hot fire in four quarts of boiling water for fifteen minutes, or until the grains can be mashed between the fingers. Strain through a colander.

15

BREAKFAST
- Hothouse raspberries with cream
- Boiled eggs
- Dry toast
- Coffee

LUNCHEON
- Livermore salad
- Fillet of halibut, Mornay
- French pastry
- Rolls
- Tea

DINNER
- Potato and leek soup
- Queen olives
- Black bass, Cambacérès
- Vol au vent Toulouse
- Roast lamb, mint sauce
- Rissolées potatoes
- Field salad
- Vanilla ice cream

Lady fingers

Coffee

Livermore salad. Broil three country sausages, allow to cool and slice thin. Mix with one peeled tomato cut in small squares, one-half cup of string beans, chives, chervil, salt and pepper, and one-third of white wine vinegar to two-thirds of olive oil.

Fillet of halibut, Mornay. Place the halibut fillets in buttered pan, season with salt and pepper, cover with fish stock or water, and boil. When nearly done remove from pan and put on buttered platter, cover with Mornay sauce, sprinkle with grated cheese and place small pieces of butter on top. Bake in oven till nice and brown. See sauce below.

Sauce Mornay. For four persons use one pint of thick cream, season with salt and Cayenne pepper, bind with the yolks of two eggs and one tablespoonful of grated cheese.

Mint sauce. Use one-quarter pound of brown sugar to one quart of vinegar. Bring to the boiling point, cool off and add some fresh mint leaves chopped fine.

Rissolées potatoes. Cut potatoes in the form of a small egg or a ball. Boil for seven minutes, then put in pan with butter and brown. Sprinkle with salt.

Vol au vent, Toulouse. Boiled breast of chicken cut in small squares; chicken dumplings, dessertspoon size; one can of French mushrooms, whole; one sliced truffle, and two sweetbreads sliced and boiled in chicken broth. Put all in casserole, add one-half wine glass of dry sherry wine, allow to become hot, and add sauce Allemande to cover. It will now be like a stew. Season to taste and fill the heated "vol au vents," or patties.

Black bass, Cambacérès. Simmer six finely chopped shallots in butter. While hot add three sliced fresh mushrooms, one peeled tomato cut in squares, and one-half glass of white wine. Reduce almost dry. Then add one pint of white wine sauce. Cook the fish "au vin blanc" style and pour the sauce over same.

BREAKFAST
  Sliced pineapple
  Rolled oats with cream
  Rolls
  Coffee

LUNCHEON
  Omelette Lorraine
  Cold lamb with jelly
  Salade Américaine
  French pancake
  Coffee

DINNER
  Potage Flamande
  Boiled codfish, sauce Horose
  Potatoes nature
  Tenderloin of beef, Bristol
  Lettuce salad
  Ice cream
  Assorted cakes
  Demi tasse

Omelette Lorraine. Serve the omelette with small sausages, broiled bacon and Madeira sauce.

Salade Américaine. Parboil one-half cup of okra cut in pieces one inch long. Peel a tomato and a boiled potato and cut in strips. Put in bowl with the okra, which has been allowed to cool, and garnish the top with very finely chopped Virginia ham over one half, and with chopped green peppers over the other half. Serve with French dressing.

Pancakes. For two persons take three-fourths of a cup of flour, the same of milk, one egg and a pinch of salt. Mix together into a thin batter. Bake on a pancake pan, well buttered.

English pancakes. Mix and cook the cakes as above. Stack one on another in a chafing dish, sprinkling each with a little lime juice and powdered sugar.

Pancakes Lieb. Same as above, but instead of the lime juice, spread each cake with sweet butter and powdered sugar. Keep hot with chafing dish.

French pancakes. Same ingredients as above, but cover each cake with currant jelly and roll into a roll. Sprinkle with powdered sugar and burn with a redhot iron in stripes.

Potage Flamande. Potato soup garnished with brunoise.

Boiled codfish, sauce Horose. Boil the codfish, place on napkin, garnish with small boiled potatoes, quartered lemons and parsley. See sauce below.

Sauce Horose. Two-thirds Hollandaise sauce and one-third tomato sauce mixed.

Tenderloin of beef, Bristol. Roast tenderloin of beef, sauce Madère, garnished with rice croquettes in pear form, purée of green peas and Laurette potatoes.

Rice croquettes. Put two ounces of butter and a finely chopped onion in vessel and simmer until yellow. Then add one cup of washed rice, one-half cup of bouillon and a pinch of salt, and cook in oven for ten minutes. Then add one cup of sauce Allemande and again put in oven for twenty minutes. When rice is well done bind with the yolks of two eggs and one spoonful of grated Parmesan cheese. Allow to cool and roll in the shape of a pear or ball or other desired shape. Bread and fry in swimming lard.

BREAKFAST
  Sliced oranges
  Boiled eggs
  Corn muffins

LUNCHEON
  Consommé Rivoli
  Olives
  Kingfish, meunière

English breakfast tea

Loin of mutton, charcutière
Corn fritters
Mashed potatoes
Coffee éclairs
Demi tasse

DINNER

Cream of chicken, à la Reine
Celery   Salted pecans
Fillet of sole, Maximilian
Roast chicken, Rosabelle
Escarole salad
Frozen raisin punch
Lady fingers
Coffee

Consommé Rivoli. Consommé garnished with carrots cut in half moon shape and boiled in consommé, small chicken dumplings and royal custard also cut in half moon shape.

Kingfish, meunière. Wash and dry the fish and season with salt and pepper. Roll in flour and sauté in pan with butter. When done put on platter and cover with sauce meunière. Garnish with quartered lemons and parsley. See sauce below.

Sauce meunière. This is a butter sauce and is principally used for fish. Place the fish or meat on a platter and sprinkle with a little salt and pepper, chopped parsley and the juice of a lemon. Heat in frying pan four ounces of butter to a hazelnut color and pour over the dish.

Loin of mutton, charcutière. Salt and pepper the loin well on the inside, and roll up. Put in roasting pan and roast in the usual manner. To make charcutière use the mutton pan gravy, or take Madeira sauce, and add two sliced pickles and one dozen sliced green olives.

Corn fritters. One-half cup of flour, one egg, one-half cup of milk, one teaspoonful of baking powder and salt and pepper. Mix well and then add one and one-half cups of grated fresh corn, or a can of drained corn. Fry in pan with hot butter. Serve on napkin.

Cream of chicken, à la Reine. Cream of chicken served with small chicken dumplings.

Fillet of sole, Maximilian. Cook fish as for "au vin blanc." Cover with Hollandaise sauce mixed with one tablespoonful of hot meat extract.

Roast chicken, Rosabelle. Garnish the chicken with hearts of artichokes and whole tomatoes, Macédoine. Sauce Madère. This garnish is fine with most any kind of meat.

Frozen raisin punch. Strain the juice of three lemons, add one pint of water, one-half pound of granulated sugar and freeze in the usual manner. Have ready one-half pound of boiled in sugar, and chopped, seeded or seedless raisins. Let the raisins cool, and add with the whites of two eggs, well beaten, to the contents of the freezer, and finish. Serve in glasses with kirschwasser or maraschino poured over the top.

18

BREAKFAST
 Wheat cakes
 Honey
 Rolls
 Coffee

LUNCHEON
 Omelette du Czar
 Pickled ham with red cabbage
 Rolled oats pudding
 Coffee

DINNER
 Purée of white beans
 Pickles
 Striped bass, Portugaise
 Braised beef

>   Macaroni in cream
>   Chiffonnade salad
>   Oriental cup
>   Cakes
>   Coffee

Omelette du Czar. Grate a horseradish root and place in pan with piece of butter. When hot add one-half cup of cream sauce and mix well. Make the omelet, and before turning on the platter put the horseradish in the center. Serve with cream sauce around the edge.

Pickled ham. Take a fresh leg of pork, rub with salt and pepper and put in earthern jar. Cover with red or white wine, or water mixed with wine, as you prefer; one onion, one carrot, a piece of celery, parsley in branches, a few pepper berries and a bouquet garni. After two or three days take out the leg of pork and roast in the ordinary manner. Half of the pork pickle may be used to make a flour gravy if desired.

Red cabbage. Slice a head of red cabbage very fine. Put in vessel with salt, pepper, one glassful of red wine and two cups of fat bouillon. Cover and cook in oven for two hours.

Red cabbage, German style. One sliced red cabbage, one-half glass of vinegar, three sliced apples, two cups of bouillon, and a small piece of salt pork or bacon. Put in oven and cook as above.

Purée of white beans. Soak two pounds of white beans over night. Put in pot and cover with stock or bouillon. Cook until soft, strain through fine sieve, put back in pot and add enough bouillon to make a soup. Season to taste, add two ounces of sweet butter, and serve with small squares of bread fried in butter, separate.

Striped bass, Portugaise. Take a whole bass and cut in slices two inches thick. Put in a buttered pan one-half of an onion chopped, three chopped shallots, a little chopped garlic and parsley, two tomatoes cut in small squares and a bouquet garni. Place the fish on top, season with salt and pepper, add one glass of white wine, one cup of stock or fish broth, cover and cook slowly. When done remove the bouquet, place the fish on platter and reduce the broth one-half. Add four ounces of butter, mix well and pour over the fish. Sprinkle with a little fresh-chopped parsley mixed with a little finely chopped garlic.

Macaroni in cream. Boil the macaroni in salt water. When done drain, add cream sauce, a little sweet butter, salt and Cayenne pepper. Serve grated cheese separate.

19

BREAKFAST
Picked-up codfish in cream
Rolls
Coffee

LUNCHEON
Grapefruit with maraschino
Poached eggs, à l'Indienne
Nivernaise salad
German huckleberry pie
Coffee

DINNER
Oysters on half shell
Clam broth in cups
Salted almonds
Boiled whitefish, Golfin
Hollandaise potatoes
Salade Rejane
Pistache ice cream
Assorted cakes
Coffee

Picked-up codfish in cream. Soak one pound of codfish in cold water over night. Cut two fresh-boiled potatoes in small squares. Put the codfish in cold water and boil for ten minutes, drain, and shred the fish in small pieces. Put in pot with the potatoes, add two cups of cream sauce, salt and a little Cayenne pepper, and simmer for ten minutes.

Poached eggs, à l'Indienne. Lay hot poached eggs on plain boiled rice and cover with curry sauce.

Curry sauce. Simmer one onion, one leek, a small piece of celery, one bay leaf, a branch of thyme and a little garlic in three ounces of butter. Then add two spoonsful of curry powder and two of flour. When hot add one quart of stock, one sliced apple, one sliced banana sauté in butter, and one-half cup of Indian chutney. Boil for twenty minutes, strain through a fine sieve and salt to taste. This sauce is used for chicken, fish, oysters, lamb, veal, etc., and should be made respectively with chicken broth, fish broth, juice of oysters, and so forth.

Salade Nivernaise. Cut in dices cooked carrots, beets and turnips. Place in salad bowl in separate piles with a bouquet of watercress in center. Season with French dressing.

Boiled whitefish, Golfin. Boil in the same manner as codfish. Serve on napkin, garnished with parsley, lemon and small boiled potatoes. Serve sauce separate. See below.

Sauce Golfin. White wine sauce mixed with small strips of boiled smoked tongue and gherkins.

Salade Rejane. Boiled celery root and artichoke buttons, and two tomatoes cut in squares. Place in salad bowl in separate piles. Slice two pimentos and place in center. Season with French dressing.

Pistache ice cream. Prepare a vanilla ice cream mixture. Crush one-quarter pound of pistachio nuts to a very fine paste, mix with a little orange flower water and two ounces of sugar. Infuse in the vanilla ice cream mixture, and strain when hot. Allow to become cold, color a very light green, and freeze.

BREAKFAST	LUNCHEON
Sliced bananas	Consommé Orleans

Shredded wheat biscuit with cream
Dry toast
Tea

Poached eggs, Diane
Tripe à la Créole
Boiled rice
Demi tasse
Coffee éclairs

DINNER

Potage Alexandra
Fish patties, Bagration
Veal kidney roast
Turnips glacés
Gendarmes potatoes
Celery root, field and beet salad
Bavarois au chocolat
Macaroons
Coffee

Consommé Orleans. Boiled barley well-washed so it will not discolor the soup, small chicken dumplings, peas, one peeled tomato cut in very small squares, and some chopped chervil. Put in consommé just before dishing up.

Poached eggs, Diane. Line a tartelette mould with paste and fill with raw white beans to support the walls, and bake in oven. Then throw out the beans and fill with tomatoes sauté in butter, place a poached egg on top, cover with Hollandaise sauce, and put in hot oven for a second.

Tripe à la Créole. Cut two pounds of boiled tripe in strips, put in casserole one pint of Créole sauce and boil for thirty minutes. Serve with boiled rice.

Potage Alexandra. Half velouté of chicken and half cream of potatoes.

Veal kidney roast. Secure a loin of veal with the kidneys left in, roll, season well and roast in the same manner as shoulder of veal.

Fish patties, Bagration. Small pieces of sole, twelve oysters, and twelve Little Neck clams boiled in white wine. Drain and add six heads of French mushrooms sliced, one sliced truffle, and enough white wine sauce to make the consistency of a stew. Have the patty shells very hot, and fill.

Turnips glacés. Cut the turnips in pieces four times the size of an almond, and put to boil in salt water. When nearly done drain, add a small piece of butter and put in oven until yellow. Then add one spoonful of meat extract and glacé them.

Gendarme potatoes. Cut the potatoes in the same shape as for French fried. Put in pan with piece of butter and roast in oven. When half done add one sliced onion and finish roasting. Sprinkle with salt and chopped parsley before serving.

Celery root, field and beet salad. Boil two peeled celery roots. When cold slice and put in salad bowl with field salad on top, and decorate with sliced boiled beets. Season with French dressing.

21

BREAKFAST
  Stewed rhubarb
  Boiled eggs
  Dipped toast
  Rolls
  Coffee

LUNCHEON
  Sweet-and-sour bananas
  Consommé Massenet
  Blood pudding
  Mashed turnips
  Camembert cheese
  Crackers
  Coffee

DINNER
  Potage Reine Margot
  Celery
  Boiled salmon, sauce Riche

Olivette potatoes
Breast of chicken, Alexandra
Hearts of lettuce
Philadelphia ice cream
Assorted cakes
Coffee

Sweet-and-sour bananas. Put six ounces of brown sugar and some pepper berries tied in cheese cloth, in one quart of vinegar and bring to the boiling point. Then add three sliced green peppers and boil for two minutes, add six sliced pimentos and remove the pepper berries. Peel one dozen bananas and put them in an earthern jar and pour the boiling vinegar and peppers over them. Let stand for twelve hours and serve cold.

Consommé Massenet. Garnish the consommé with boiled carrots cut in half-moon shape, and boiled macaroni cut in pieces one-half inch long. Sprinkle with chopped chervil.

Blood pudding. Made of pork blood, etc., and may be obtained from your butcher. Broil or fry in butter.

Potage Reine Margot. To cream of chicken add some almonds mashed fine, mixed with a little cream, and strained. This is called almond milk.

Sauce Riche. Mix a tablespoonful of anchovy paste with a pint of Hollandaise sauce, add one truffle, three heads of French mushrooms, and one dozen shrimps cut in small squares.

Breast of chicken, Alexandra. Take the breasts of a raw roasting chicken, season with salt and pepper, put in sauté pan with butter. Cook until nice and yellow, add one-half cup of cream and finish cooking. Place the breasts on two oval croustades filled with string beans sauté. Add the cream gravy to a cup of Mornay sauce, with a little paprika, cover the breasts with this sauce and bake in oven till golden yellow. Serve on napkin with parsley in branches.

Vanilla Bavarois. Boil one quart of milk with one-half of a split vanilla bean. Stir in gradually, until it gets creamy, six ounces of sugar mixed with the yolks of four eggs. Add five leaves of gelatine that have been washed in cold water, stirring until melted. Strain, when cold add one pint of rich, very stiff, whipped cream. Pour into moulds of fancy shape and place in ice box for about two hours. Serve with vanilla sauce or sweetened whipped cream flavored with vanilla.

BREAKFAST
- Baked apples with cream
- Scrambled eggs with fine herbes
- Crescents
- Coffee

LUNCHEON
- Croustade Cancalaise
- Consommé Fleury
- Ragout à la Deutsch
- Roquefort cheese
- Crackers
- Coffee

DINNER
- Potage Faubonne
- Médaillon of sole, St. Victor
- Roast squab
- Asparagus Hollandaise
- Duchesse potatoes
- Romaine salad
- Pineapple water ice
- Assorted cakes
- Coffee

Scrambled eggs with fine herbs. Add to the eggs some fine cut chives, parsley and chervil.

Croustade Cancalaise. Drain off the juice from pickled oysters and fill the croustades with them. Cover with sauce Tyrolienne and garnish with chopped hard-boiled eggs.

Consommé Fleury. Sliced sorrel boiled in water for a second, boiled rice, small asparagus tips and peas, in equal parts. Serve in consommé.

Ragout à la Deutsch. One-half pound of sliced raw tenderloin of beef, and three lamb kidneys, season with salt and pepper and fry in frying pan with very hot butter. When done remove the meat and place in a deep dish. Put three chopped shallots and a green pepper cut in small dices, in the butter in frying pan and simmer for a minute. Drain, add two cups of brown gravy and one cup of sauté potatoes. Mix with the meat, but do not allow to boil. Serve from the deep dish or casserole.

Potage Faubonne. Make a purée of white beans and bind with the yolk of one egg mixed with a little cream. Serve small squares of bread fried in butter, separate.

Médaillon of sole, St. Victor. Cook the fish in white wine and allow to become cold. Mix the stock with white wine sauce, bring to a boil and reduce until it becomes very thick. Strain and mix with equal parts of mayonnaise, whipping well so it will not turn. Let the sauce become cold and pour over the fish, and place in the ice box. Boil three eggs for seven minutes, cool, split in two crosswise, remove the yolk and fill with fresh caviar. Turn the eggs upside down and cover with some of the fish sauce, colored a delicate rose. Cut some peeled tomatoes in the form of strawberries, and make a vegetable salad mixed with a little thick mayonnaise. Make a pyramid of the salad in the middle of the dish, place the fillet of sole around it, and garnish with the eggs and tomatoes. Sprinkle with chopped parsley.

BREAKFAST
  Honey in comb
  Waffles
  Yarmouth bloater
  Rolls
  Coffee

LUNCHEON
  German pancakes
  Chocolate
  Whipped cream

DINNER
  Potage Mathilda
  Lobster croquettes, cream sauce
  Plain potted squab chicken
  Stewed tomatoes
  Lettuce braisé
  Château potatoes
  Cold artichokes, mustard sauce
  Charlotte aux pommes
  Coffee

German pancakes. Two eggs, one-half cup of milk, one-half cup of flour, a pinch of salt, a little nutmeg and one teaspoonful of sugar. Mix well. Have a large frying pan ready with hot butter. Be sure and have the butter run all over the inside of the pan so the pancake will not stick to the sides when it rises. Pour in the batter and place in oven. When nearly done, powder with sugar and put back in oven to brown. Serve with lemon and powdered sugar.

Potage Mathilda. Cream of cucumbers with small squares of bread fried in butter.

Rice Créole. Put in sauce pan three ounces of butter, one chopped onion, a slice of raw ham cut in small squares, and one green pepper cut in small dices. Simmer until the onions are soft, then add one cup of washed rice, one peeled and chopped tomato, two red peppers (pimentos), cut in small dices, two cups of stock or bouillon, and a little salt. Cover and put in oven until the rice is soft. Before serving add two spoonsful of grated Parmesan or Swiss cheese. This rice may be used for stuffing green peppers, tomatoes, onions, etc.

Chicken croquettes. Three cups of chicken hash made from white and dark meat, one cup of chopped fresh or canned mushrooms, and one-half onion chopped very fine. Simmer in butter. Then add two cups of Allemande or cream sauce, season with salt and Cayenne pepper. Put on fire and reduce until thick. Bind with the yolks of two eggs. Allow to become cold, and form in pyramid shape or in the shape of a large cork, bread, and fry in swimming fat until well colored. Serve on napkin with sauce separate, or around the croquettes. A chopped truffle may be added before simmering, if desired.

Sweetbread croquettes. Three cups of sweetbreads parboiled and cut in small dices, and if desired, one chopped truffle. Simmer with chopped onions, and then follow recipe for chicken croquettes.

Lobster croquettes. Three cups of lobster cut in small dices, one cup of canned or fresh mushrooms, and one truffle chopped fine. Simmer all in butter, then add one-half glass of sherry wine and cook for two minutes, then add two cups of cream sauce and reduce. Bind with the yolks of three eggs. Follow directions for chicken croquettes for cooking and serving.

BREAKFAST	LUNCHEON
Preserved figs with cream	Petite marmite
Shirred eggs	Broiled lobster
Dry toast	Roast beef
Cocoa	Cléo potatoes

String bean salad

Lemon pie

Coffee

DINNER

Potage Duchesse

Fillet of sole, Marguery

Roast lamb, mint sauce

Succotash

Broiled fresh mushrooms on toast

Alligator pear salad

Peach Tetrazzini

Assorted cakes

Coffee

Petite marmite. Put in a vessel with cold water to cover, five pounds of short ribs of beef and a soup hen. Season with a spoonful of salt, and bring to a boil, and skim carefully so the broth will be clear. Then add two large carrots, three turnips, a piece of cabbage, one stalk of celery and four leeks, all tied in a cheese cloth; one bouquet garni, and a large marrow bone. When beef and fowl are well done remove, take off the skin and fat and cut the meat in pieces one inch square. Remove the bouquet garni, and cut the cabbage, carrots, turnips, celery and leeks in round pieces one-half inch in diameter. Put the beef, chicken and vegetables in another pot and strain the broth over them. Boil slowly for five minutes. Have your butcher saw some raw marrow bones in wafers as thin as paper, and add them to the soup at the last moment. Serve very hot in soup tureen, with a sprinkle of chopped chervil. Cut some crust of bread or rolls in diamond shape, bake in oven till brown, and serve separate. Special earthern petite marmite pots are carried at the large stores, and are preferable to tureens for serving.

Broiled lobster. Cut a live lobster in two lengthwise, season with salt and pepper, sprinkle with olive oil, and broil on hot iron. Serve with maître d'hôtel sauce, garnished with lemons and parsley.

Cléo potatoes. Cut raw potatoes in pear shapes the size of an egg, parboil in salt water, then put in a well-buttered pan pointed end up, sprinkle with melted butter and roast in oven, basting all the time till brown. When done, salt and serve on napkin, garnished with parsley.

String bean salad. Put in salad bowl some cold boiled string beans, sprinkle with very finely-sliced chives, chopped parsley, salt and fresh-ground black pepper, and one-third vinegar and two-thirds olive oil.

Potage Duchesse. Cream of rice with royal in strips.

Fillet of sole, Marguery. Prepare the sole as for "au vin blanc." Place on top of each fillet two parboiled mussels, and two heads of French mushrooms, cover with sauce "au vin blanc," sprinkle with bread crumbs made from stale rolls, and a little butter, and bake in hot oven until a light yellow color.

25

BREAKFAST
- Hothouse raspberries with cream
- Oatmeal
- Rolls
- Coffee

LUNCHEON
- Eggs ministerielle
- Cold assorted meats
- Chiffonnade salad
- Pont Neuf cake
- Demi tasse

DINNER
- Blue Points, mignonette
- Bisque d'écrevisses
- Salted almonds   Celery
- Ripe California olives
- Fillet of trout, Café de Paris
- Sweetbreads braisé, au jus

      Purée de marrons
      Roast goose, apple sauce
      Sweet potatoes, Southern style
      Pâté de foie gras de Strasbourg
      Lettuce salad, aux fines herbes
      Frozen diplomate pudding
      Assorted cakes
      Pont l'évêque cheese Crackers
      Nuts and raisins Coffee

Eggs ministerielle. Cut sandwich bread in slices about two inches thick. With a round cutter about three inches in diameter cut out the white of the bread. With another cutter about an inch and a half in diameter cut out the center of the round slices, leaving a ring of bread. Soak these rings in thick cream for a second, put on buttered dish, break an egg in the center of each, salt and pepper, cover with a light cream sauce, sprinkle with grated cheese, and bake in oven for about eight minutes.

Pont Neuf potatoes. Three times the size of regular "French" fried potatoes.

Sweetbreads braisé au jus. (Glacé). Place in buttered sauté pan one sliced onion, one carrot, a little parsley, a bay leaf and a clove, and a few pepper berries. Put three parboiled sweetbreads, which may be larded with fresh or salted pork if desired, on top, add one-half cup of bouillon, salt, and put over fire to boil. When reduced place in oven, add a small quantity of meat extract, and glacé by basting continually with its own broth, until well browned. When done lay on platter and strain the broth over them.

Bisque d'écrevisses. Remove the tails of three dozen écrevisses. Use two-thirds of the shells, broken up, to make the soup, and one-third for écrevisse butter. Simmer in butter one onion, one carrot, a leek and a little celery, all cut up; with one bay leaf, some thyme and one spoonful of black pepper berries. Then add the broken shells, two spoonsful of flour, one glass of white wine, one-half glass of brandy, one gallon of bouillon and one cup of raw rice. Season with salt and Cayenne pepper, cook till rice is very soft, and strain through fine sieve. Bisque should be a little thicker than other cream soups. Before serving add two spoonsful of écrevisse butter and stir well, then add the écrevisse tails and one-half glass of Cognac.

Écrevisse butter. Break fine in mortar some écrevisse (crayfish) shells. Put in sauce pan with one-half pound of butter, one-half onion, one-half carrot, a small piece of celery, one-half of a leek stalk, a little thyme, one bay leaf and a few pepper berries, and simmer in oven till butter is clarified, or clear, and all the other liquids evaporated. Squeeze through cheese cloth into a bowl standing in ice. The butter will rise to the top, and may be easily removed when cold. This butter is used with many sauces, soups, etc.

Lobster butter. Use lobster shells and prepare in the same manner as écrevisse butter. This butter is used for lobster sauce, Newburg dishes, soups, etc.

26

BREAKFAST
- Stewed prunes
- Boiled eggs
- Toast
- Tea

LUNCHEON
- Grapefruit en suprême
- Cold goose and ham, apple sauce
- Romaine salad
- Brie cheese
- Crackers
- Coffee

DINNER
- Potage bonne femme
- Roast ruddy duck
- Fried hominy and currant jelly
- Cold asparagus, mustard sauce
- Baba au rhum

Coffee

Potage bonne femme. Purée of white beans with Julienne of vegetables.

Fillet of sole, Florentine. Put the fillet of one sole in a buttered pan, salt, add one-half glass of water mixed with white wine, and boil until done. In the center of a buttered platter put a cup of purée of spinach and place the boiled fillet on top, cover with Mornay sauce, with grated cheese and small bits of butter on top of the sauce. Bake in oven until brown.

Roast ruddy duck. Roast for twelve minutes, in the same manner as teal duck.

Baba au rhum. One-half pound of flour, one ounce of yeast, three ounces of butter, two ounces of sugar, two ounces of currants and the rind and juice of one lemon. Dissolve the yeast in one cup of warm milk and make a soft sponge with half of the flour, cover and let rise in a warm place. Work the sugar and the butter together until creamy, add the eggs and lemon and the rest of the flour. When the sponge has risen to twice its original size mix with the batter; at the same time adding the currants. Fill baba moulds half full and let raise until nearly to the edge of the moulds. Bake in a rather hot oven. When done soak well in a syrup made with one pint of water, one pound of sugar, one gill of rum and the juice of a lemon. Pour some of the sauce over the babas when serving.

Savarin au kirsch. Make a dough the same as for baba au rhum, but omit the currants. Fill a round crown-shaped savarin mould half full, allow to raise, and bake. Soak in a syrup made of one pint of water, one pound of sugar, and one gill of kirschwasser. Serve warm.

Savarin Chantilly. Same as savarin au kirsch, but decorated with whipped cream, and served cold.

Savarin Montmorency. Like savarin au kirsch, but serve hot with stewed stoned cherries as sauce.

Savarin mirabelle. Same as savarin au kirsch, but serve hot with stewed stoned mirabelles.

BREAKFAST
  Preserved figs
  Ham and eggs
  Toasted corn muffins
  Coffee

LUNCHEON
  Consommé in cups
  Ripe olives
  Panfish sauté, meunière
  Stewed tripe, Blanchard
  Savarin au kirsch   Coffee

DINNER
  Potage Flamande
  Frogs' legs, sauté à sec
  Roast sirloin of beef, Porte Maillot
  Lettuce braisé
  Château potatoes
  Endive salad
  Biscuit glacé
  Assorted cakes
  Coffee

Stewed tripe, Blanchard. Simmer a chopped onion in three ounces of butter, add one pint of bouillon, or stock, or chicken broth, one spoonful of flour, one pound of tripe cut in strips, one cupful of raw round potatoes cut out with a small-size "Parisian" spoon, one bouquet garni and one gill of white wine. Cover and cook for one hour, or until potatoes are very soft. Before serving remove bouquet garni and sprinkle with fresh-chopped parsley.

Potage Flamande. Potato soup mixed with brunoise.

Frogs' legs, sauté à sec. To have the best flavor frogs should be killed just before cooking. Remove the skins and cut off the hind legs, salt and pepper them and roll in flour. Sauté one dozen frogs' legs in three ounces of hot butter in a frying pan, for a few minutes over a good fire. Then add a chopped shallot and let simmer for a few minutes. The legs should then be crisp. Serve on a platter with chopped parsley and lemon.

Roast sirloin of beef, Porte Maillot. Roast the sirloin, serve with sauce Madère, garnish with small French carrots, celery braisé, lettuce braisé and château potatoes.

Lettuce braisé. Wash four heads of large romaine lettuce in cold water, parboil in salt water, cool, and squeeze dry with the hands. Cut each head in four lengthwise, remove the stem, season with salt and pepper, and fold so both ends come together. Place a piece of pigskin in the bottom of a buttered pan, put the lettuce on top, and add a sliced onion, one carrot and a bay leaf. Cover with buttered manilla paper and allow to simmer for a while. Then add one cup of stock, put in oven and cook until soft. Used for garnishing entrées, etc.

Biscuit glacé. Put in double boiler eight yolks of eggs, one-half pound of sugar, and one-half of a split vanilla bean. Cook until it thickens, stirring continually. Then remove from the fire and beat with an egg whip until cold and very light. Remove the vanilla bean, add one quart of whipped cream and mix lightly. Put in fancy paper cases or fancy moulds, and freeze. Before serving decorate the tops with whipped cream, or any kind of ice cream or water ice.

Biscuit glacé, St. Francis. Fill some oblong paper cases with biscuit glacé foundation, put in ice box to freeze, decorate the tops with pistachio and strawberry ice cream before serving.

Biscuit glacé of strawberry, raspberry, coffee, pistachio, chocolate, apple, mapleine, pineapple, kirsch, peppermint, etc. Same as Biscuit Glacé, but decorate with the desired ice cream or water ice before serving.

BREAKFAST	LUNCHEON
Broiled Finnan haddie	Canapé of sardines

Baked potatoes   Boston baked beans
Rolls   Brown bread
Coffee   Coffee

DINNER

Seapuit oysters

Cream of rice

Salted pecans

Fillet of flounder, Café Riche

Spring lamb tenderloin, Thomas

Roast chicken, au jus

Hearts of romaine, egg dressing

Strawberry parfait

Macaroons

Coffee

Broiled Finnan haddie. (Smoked haddock). Remove the bones, roll in oil and put on iron to broil. When done on both sides place on platter, cover with maître d'hôtel sauce or plain melted butter, garnish with parsley in branches and quartered lemons.

Cream of rice. Melt in sauce pan two ounces of butter, add one-quarter pound of rice flour, and when hot, one and one-half pints of chicken broth. Boil for ten minutes and strain. Season with salt and Cayenne pepper, and add one-half pint of hot cream and a small piece of butter before serving.

Salted Pecans. Roast one-half pound of shelled pecans to a light brown color, wet with a solution of water and a little gum Arabic, or the white of an egg, while they are still hot, and then dust over with one spoonful of fine table salt and stir until dry.

Salted English walnuts. Follow directions for pecans.

Fillet of flounder, Café Riche. Put the fillets in a buttered pan, cover with white wine, and boil. When done place on platter, pour Génoise sauce with the addition of a spoonful of beef extract, over the fish.

Spring lamb tenderloin, Thomas. Broil the tenderloin and dish up on buttered toast, and cover with sauce Colbert. Garnish on one side with small boiled potatoes covered with cream sauce, and flageolet beans on the other.

Flageolet beans. These are French beans and can be obtained in cans. Put on the fire in salt water, bring to the boiling point, and drain. Add sweet butter, salt and pepper, mix well and serve immediately.

Egg dressing, for salads. Chop two hard-boiled eggs, and put in salad bowl with one-half teaspoonful of French mustard, one pinch of salt, some fresh-ground pepper, a little chopped parsley, a little chervil, two spoonsful of vinegar and four of olive oil. Mix well.

Strawberry parfait. With one quart of strawberry ice cream mix one pint of sweet whipped cream. Put in moulds or glasses and serve with whipped cream on top.

Parfaits. Pistachio, vanilla, chocolate, peach and café, all prepared the same as strawberry.

Neapolitan parfait. Put in mould or glass, three kinds of parfaits, as strawberry, vanilla and pistachio. Allow to become very hard in ice box, and serve whipped cream on top.

Wilson parfait. Peach parfait with the addition of some chopped peeled peaches. Serve with whipped cream and a crystallized violet on top.

BREAKFAST
  Baked apples
  Oatmeal with cream
  Rolls

LUNCHEON
  Canapé Monte Carlo
  Poached eggs, Persanne
  Tosca salad

Coffee	French pastry
Coffee

DINNER

Consommé Madrilène
Ripe California olives
Boiled salmon, sauce Anglaise
Ragout fin
Stanislaus salad
Cream cheese with Bar le Duc
Crackers
Coffee

Canapé Monte Carlo. Purée of foie gras lightly mixed with a little stiff mayonnaise and spread on thin toast. Garnish around the edge with chopped yolks of hard-boiled eggs, and serve on napkins with parsley in branches.

Eggs Persanne. Place hot poached eggs on a round toast, cover with tomato sauce and sprinkle with fine chopped ham and parsley.

Tosca salad. Cut in fine strips about one inch long some boiled ham, tongue, cooked potatoes and buttons of artichokes. Arrange in salad bowl with some asparagus tips in the center, garnish with the chopped yolks and whites of hard-boiled eggs, separate; and serve with French dressing.

Consommé Madrilène. Slice a handful of sorrel and cook for five minutes in consommé. Add vermicelli and one tomato cut in small dices. Serve grated cheese separate.

Boiled salmon, sauce Anglaise. Cook the salmon in the same manner as for Hollandaise. For sauce Anglaise use one pint of Hollandaise sauce, mixed with two chopped hard-boiled eggs, sliced chives, chopped parsley and chervil. Serve separate.

Stanislaus salad. Remove the inside leaves of a whole head of lettuce, leaving a green bowl. Put in bottom, celery cut in long strips, with slices of grapefruit and seedless grapes cut in half, on top. Sprinkle with chopped walnuts. Serve with French dressing.

Ragout fin. Slice some parboiled tender sweetbreads, chickens' livers, chickens' combs, chickens' kidneys and truffles, and sauté in butter, cooking each separately. Then put all in one pan, add a half glass of good sherry, boil for one minute, add a half pint of brown gravy, simmer for a few minutes, and serve with chopped chervil on top. Chickens' combs and kidneys come in bottles from France. If you wish you may cut the tips from raw rooster combs, put in boiling water for a minute, when they can be rubbed with salt to remove the skin. Then soak in cold water to cause the blood to run out, and boil in salt water till soft.

Cream cheese with Bar le Duc. Mix some cream cheese with a little whipped cream and spread on plate in the shape of a ring. Put some red Bar le Duc jelly in center. Serve toasted crackers separate.

30

BREAKFAST
  Grapefruit
  Pork sausages Apple
  sauce
  Wheat cakes   Coffee

LUNCHEON
  Plain consommé in cups
  Fried fillet of sole, rémoulade
  Brie cheese and
    crackers   Coffee

DINNER
  Potage Jackson   Crab meat Monza
  Chicken dumplings, sauce Allemande
  Braised beef à la mode   Peas à la Français
  Duchesse potatoes
  Pineapple biscuit glacé
  Assorted cakes   Coffee

Fried fillet of sole. Clean and trim the fillets, season with salt and pepper, roll in flour, then in beaten eggs, then in bread crumbs, and fry in swimming hot lard for five minutes. Remove and serve on napkin with quartered lemons and fried parsley. Sauce separate.

Rémoulade sauce. Take a handful of spinach, one of watercress and one of parsley and mash fine in a mortar. Put in a cloth and press out the juice. Mix the juice with a pint and a half of mayonnaise, add four chopped gherkins and some sliced chives.

Crab meat, Monza. Wash carefully one pound of fresh mushrooms, and cut each one in four. Put in sauté pan with two ounces of butter and simmer for thirty minutes. When the mushrooms are soft add the meat of one crab cooked in cream. Before serving add one gill of dry sherry wine.

Crab meat in cream. Remove the meat from the shell of a boiled crab. In a sauce pan put a piece of butter the size of an egg, and place on stove. When warm add two spoonsful of flour and allow to become hot, then add one pint of boiling milk and one-fourth of a pint of hot cream. Stir well and boil for ten minutes. Season with salt and Cayenne pepper, then add the crab meat and serve in deep dish. Serve dry toast separate.

Chicken dumplings. (Quenelles de volaille). Take the breast of a raw fowl and trim carefully away the fat, using the white meat only. Chop very fine and pass through a fine sieve, place in a bowl on ice, season with salt and Cayenne pepper, and with a wooden spoon stir in little by little some very thick cream (not whipped), which has been kept on ice. Add the cream until you have nearly double the amount of force meat. Have two teaspoons in cold water. Take one and fill with the force meat, make a little hole in the middle and fill with goose liver purée and close up. Remove the dumpling from the first spoon with the other one and place on a buttered pan, and continue. When enough are formed cover with stock and bring to the boiling point, then set off the fire and let stand for ten minutes on the back of the range. The force meat may be used for small dumplings without the purée of goose liver; or some other filling may be used. Make them small for garnishing consommé, vol au vent, patties, financière, tortue, etc. The force meat is also used to make timbales of chicken.

Sauce Allemande. Cut up three pounds of veal bones, put in vessel with two gallons of water, bring to a boil and skim. Add one onion, a carrot, a little celery and leek, some pepper berries, two cloves, a sprig of thyme and some salt. Boil for two hours and strain. Put in sauce pan three ounces of butter, when hot add two ounces of flour and heat again. Then add a pint and a half of the broth, boil for ten minutes, season and strain. This is the foundation of many fancy sauces.

Potage Jackson. Potato soup with small pieces of macaroni added.

www.ingramcontent.com/pod-product-compliance
Lightning Source LLC
Chambersburg PA
CBHW081121080526
44587CB00021B/3695